TERROR IN THE SKIES

TERROR
IN THE SKIES

Why 9/11 Could Happen Again

ANNIE JACOBSEN

SPENCE PUBLISHING COMPANY • DALLAS

2005

Published in the United States by
Spence Publishing Company
111 Cole Street
Dallas, Texas 75207

ISBN: 1-890626-62-7
978-1-890626-62-4
Library of Congress Control Number: 2005931305

Printed in the United States of America

To Kevin and our boys.

To Alice and Tom and their forty years together.

Contents

Prologue

ON JUNE 29, 2004, my husband, my son, and I were returning home from my parents' fortieth wedding anniversary celebration in Connecticut. Our connecting flight to Los Angeles was Northwest Airlines flight 327 from Detroit. It should have been just another flight. Instead, fourteen Middle Eastern men acted as if they might hijack the plane. There were air marshals on board monitoring the tense situation, and the captain of the Boeing 757 radioed ahead for help. Just a few minutes before flight 327 landed, one of the men stood in the aisle, made a slashing motion across his neck with his hand, and mouthed the word "No."

Approximately twenty-five federal agents and local law enforcement officers met the plane at the gate. My husband and I spent the next two hours giving statements. Yet come the next morning, the story was absent from the news.

I wrote about the harrowing flight in an article called "Terror in the Skies, Again?" which was published on WomensWallStreet.com. The story spread like wildfire across the Internet and quickly became world news. Within forty-eight hours, pilots, flight attendants, and federal air marshals flooded the webzine with emails,[1] stating that what happened on flight 327 was not an isolated incident. These kinds of "dry runs" had been happening, they said, and if the government didn't do something about it, 9/11 would happen again.

The federal agencies involved in the incident defended themselves aggressively, claiming that they had conducted a thorough investigation. The men involved were nothing more than a musical band. But the story wouldn't go away—in fact, it got bigger. Ultimately, Congress got involved.

I've spent the last year investigating the tangled tale of flight 327. I've uncovered the alarming details of what happened on the flight and—alarming in another way altogether—how the government agencies involved in the investigation wanted the story to go away so badly, they went on national television and lied.

The Department of Homeland Security has also spent the last year investigating what went on during and after flight 327. And the U.S. House Judiciary Committee has spent as much time looking into the errors made by many of the federal agents involved. But these agents have stayed firm: *nothing happened* on flight 327, they claim. *Nothing happened.*

Something did happen on flight 327. And in this book, I tell what happened. I also tell what I've learned from those at high levels of government, air marshals, the media, and ordinary flyers. We can't take *nothing happened* for an answer.

Acknowledgments

T HIS BOOK WOULD NOT EXIST were in not for the support and collaborative efforts of WomensWallStreet. com. They published "Terror in the Skies, Again?" in July 2004, and from that day forward, cheered me on like nothing I could have ever expected. Pamela Little, editor in chief of the webzine, helped me craft each of the thirteen installments that followed. She has been a friend and mentor every step of the way, and to her I owe a huge debt of gratitude. If everyone had a boss like Pamela Little, more people would smile while doing their work.

Brendi Rawlin of Porter Novelli juggled the media storm like a diplomat; without her neither Pamela nor I could have enjoyed an opportunity such as this. Caryl Winter and Nancie Clare, my colleagues at the webzine who oversee all my articles, I thank you both for always offering insight, wisdom, and direction. Brian Thomas, thank you for keeping the office together and for handling the voluminous amount of email that poured in. This has been a year-long task, and you have never missed a beat. Kerry Jarrell for all you do behind the scenes, and David Bennett, CEO of WomensWallStreet. com, thank you for your unflinching support.

The book would not exist without the help of a great number of sources who gave me information, most of whom must remain anonymous. You know who you are, and I hope you witness your efforts in this book. Those who spoke on the record and whom I've mentioned in my footnotes, thank you. Certain individuals stand out among my heroes: Mr. Vegas, Poo, Vaughn Allex, David Gavigan, Tom Heidenberger, Debra Burlingame, and Frank Terreri, who handled his own tangle with the FAMS with panache. And my heartfelt thanks to my friend under the white dome.

Thanks to Mitchell Muncy, who took the first manuscript I submitted, turned it inside out, and believed that I could put it back together. This is my first book; to Spence I say thank you for making an author out of me.

Thanks to Kathleen and Keith for keeping me connected. And to Glenn, who reminded me not to get off the podium before I finished what I had to say.

My husband, Kevin Jacobsen, is my best friend, my favorite reader, my most honest editor, and the kindest person I know. I am one lucky lady to have him in my life.

Thanks to Alice and Tom Soininen, my inspirational parents, who have encouraged me to write since I was learning how to spell. My hat goes off to my mother-in-law, Marion Wroldsen, who received her first paycheck as a writer as I was writing this book—at the age of seventy-two. Allen and Mumin, thank you for your kind words and your encouragement.

TERROR IN THE SKIES

Northwest 327

ON JUNE 29, 2004, I flew on Northwest Airlines flight 327 from Detroit to Los Angeles with my husband, Kevin, and our young son. Also on our flight were fourteen Middle Eastern men between the ages of approximately twenty and fifty. What I experienced during that flight has caused me to question whether the United States of America can realistically uphold the civil liberties of every individual, including non-citizens, and still protect its citizens from terrorist threats.

On that Tuesday, our journey began uneventfully. Starting out that morning in Providence, Rhode Island, we went through security screening, flew to Detroit, and passed the time waiting for our connecting flight to Los Angeles by shopping at the airport stores and eating lunch at an airport diner. With no second security check required in Detroit,[1] we headed to our gate and waited for the pre-boarding announcement. Standing near us, also waiting to pre-board, was a group of six Middle Eastern men. They were carrying blue passports with Arabic writing. Two men wore tracksuits with Arabic writing across the back. Two carried musical instrument cases—thin, flat, eighteen inches long. The fifth man wore a yellow shirt and held a McDonald's bag. And the sixth man had a bad leg: he wore a thick-heeled orthopedic shoe, and he limped. When the pre-boarding announcement was made, we handed our tickets to the Northwest Airlines agent and walked down the jetway with the group of men directly behind us.[2]

My four-year-old son was determined to wheel his carry-on bag himself, so I turned to the men behind me and said, "You go ahead, this could be a while." "No, you go ahead," one of the men replied. He smiled pleasantly and extended his arm for me to pass. He was young, maybe late twenties, and had a goatee. I thanked him and we boarded the plane.

Once on the plane, we took our seats in the front of the coach class cabin, in the row second from the aircraft exit door (in seats 17A, 17B, and 17C). The man with the yellow shirt and the McDonald's bag sat across the aisle from us in seat 17E. The pleasant man with the goatee sat a few rows back and across the aisle from us in seat 21E. The rest of the men were seated throughout the plane, and several made their way to the back.

As we sat waiting for the passengers to finish boarding, we noticed another large group of Middle Eastern men boarding. The first man wore a dark suit and sunglasses.

He sat in first class in seat 1A, the seat second-closest to the cockpit door.[3] The other seven men walked into the coach cabin. Kevin and I exchanged glances, then continued to get comfortable. I noticed some of the other passengers paying attention as well. As boarding continued, we watched as, one by one, most of the Middle Eastern men made eye contact with each other. They continued to look at each other and nod, as if they were all in agreement about something. I could tell that Kevin was beginning to feel anxious.

He said that something was not right. He told me that he was considering having us get off the plane.

For eleven years, I had been traveling the globe with my husband—flying more than one hundred thousand miles, to Europe, Asia, and all throughout the United States. I had never seen him the slightest bit uncomfortable on any flight, about anything, or about any person.

He repeated what he had said: *We need to get off the plane. Something is not right.*

All the passengers were now seated; the flight was full. Two ground agents, standing a few feet in front of me, flipped through paperwork and hurried the flight for departure. I watched Kevin think through his decision.

Suddenly, the man with the limp and the orthopedic shoe came rushing up from the back of the plane.

"I have to switch seats!" He said loudly in heavily accented English. And again, he said, "I have to switch seats!"

"Just go sit anywhere," the male ground agent told him dismissively, waving a hand.

The ground agents left the plane; flight attendants closed the aircraft door. Kevin looked at me. "Annie," he said, "I need to fake a heart attack so we can get off this plane. Something is really wrong." The wheels unlocked and the plane was now rolling back from the gate.

I didn't say anything.

Kevin sat there thinking. The plane taxied out to the runway, and soon we were up in the air.

The take-off was uneventful. But immediately after the seatbelt sign was turned off, the unusual activity began. The man in the yellow shirt got out of his seat and went to the lavatory at the front of coach—taking his full McDonald's bag with him. When he came out of the lavatory he still had the McDonald's bag, only now it was almost empty. He walked down the aisle to the back of the plane, still holding the bag. When he passed two of the men sitting mid-cabin, he gave a thumbs-up sign. When he returned to his seat, he no longer had the McDonald's bag.

Then another man from the group stood up and took something from his carry-on in the overhead bin. It was about a foot long and was rolled in cloth. He headed toward the back of the cabin with the object. Five minutes later, several more of the Middle Eastern men began using the forward lavatory, consecutively. In the back, several of the men stood up and used the back lavatory, also consecutively.

For the next hour, the men congregated in groups of two and three at the back of the plane for varying periods of time. Meanwhile, in the first class cabin, just a foot or so from the cockpit door, the man with the dark suit—still wearing sunglasses—was also standing. Not one of the flight crew suggested to any of these men that they take their seats.

Watching all of this, Kevin was now beyond anxious. I decided to try to reassure him (and maybe myself) by walking to the back lavatory. The goateed man and I had exchanged friendly words when we boarded the plane. I knew he was seated only a few rows behind, on the other side of the aisle, and I thought I would say hello to him—to get some reassurance that everything was fine. As I stood up and turned around, I glanced in his direction, and we made eye contact. I threw out my friendliest "remember-me-we-had-a-nice-exchange-just-a-short-time-ago" smile. The man did not smile back. His face did not move. In fact, the cold, defiant look he gave me sent shivers down my spine.

As I walked to the back lavatory, I was alarmed by how many Middle Eastern men were standing back there. They had to move for me to get by. Two were standing mid-cabin. One stood outside the lavatory, stretching his legs, and another, possibly two, were standing in the galley, watching the flight attendant. I looked around the plane. Of the passengers standing, *all* were Middle Eastern men.

When I returned to my seat I was unable to assure my husband that all was well. I suggested that he talk to the flight attendant. Kevin walked into the first class cabin and spoke with a female flight attendant: "I might be overreacting, but I've been watching some really suspicious things . . ." Before he could finish his sentence, the flight attendant pulled him into the galley. In a quiet voice she explained that they were all concerned about what was going on. She said the captain was aware of it, and the flight attendants were passing notes to each other about the men. And then she said that there were people on board "higher up than you and me watching." Kevin returned to his seat. He relayed this information to me by writing it down on a piece of paper to be discreet.[4] He was feeling slightly better; I was feeling much worse. We were now two hours into a four-and-a-half hour flight.

About ten minutes later, that same flight attendant came by with the drinks cart. She leaned over and quietly told Kevin that there were federal air marshals sitting all around us.[5] She asked him not to tell anyone and explained that she could get in trouble for giving out that information. She then continued serving drinks.

About twenty minutes later, the same flight attendant returned. Leaning over and whispering, she asked Kevin to write a description of the yellow-shirted man sitting across from us. She explained that it would look too suspicious if she wrote down the information. She asked Kevin to slip the note to her when he was done, which he did.

After seeing fourteen Middle Eastern men board separately (six together, eight individually) and then act as a group, seeing their unusual glances, observing their bizarre bathroom activities, watching them congregate in small groups, knowing that the flight attendants and the pilots were seriously concerned, and now knowing that federal air marshals were on board, I was officially terrified. A month before this particular flight, I had traveled to India to do research for a magazine article I was writing on the Maharaja of Jodhpur. My husband and I flew on a jumbo jet carrying more than three hundred Hindu and Muslim men and women. We traveled throughout the country, flying on airplanes, and I stayed in a Muslim village ten miles outside Pakistan. I never once felt fearful, never once felt unsafe, never once had the feeling that anyone wanted to hurt me. This time was different.

Finally, the captain announced that the plane was cleared for landing. It had been four hours since we left Detroit. The fasten seatbelt light came on, and I could see downtown Los Angeles. The flight attendants made one final sweep of the cabin and strapped themselves in for landing. I began to relax. Home was in sight.

Suddenly, seven of the men stood up—in unison—and walked to the front and back lavatories of the coach class cabin. The gesture was overtly provocative. One by one, they went into the lavatories, each spending about four minutes inside. A few feet in front of me, around the forward lavatory, I watched as two men stood against the emergency exit door. One did a few squats, and the other stretched his arms over his head. Another stood blocking the aisle, and the fourth man remained inside the bathroom. I looked to the back of the plane, the situation was the same: two men standing next to the bathroom and blocking the aisle.

In front of me, the men spoke in Arabic among themselves and to the man in the yellow shirt sitting nearby. One of the men took his camera into the lavatory; another took his cell phone. Again, no flight attendant approached any of the men. Not one of the flight attendants asked them to sit down.

I watched the man in the yellow shirt. Still sitting in his seat, he reached inside the front of his shirt and stuck his hand all the way down into his shirt to retrieve something tucked inside his belt. He pulled out a small, red book and read a few pages. Then he put the book back inside his shirt. After a moment, he pulled the book out again, read a page or two, and put it back again. He did this several more times. There was still a man in the bathroom.

I looked around to see if any other passengers were watching. In a nearby aisle seat, a woman sat reading the bestselling novel, *Life of Pi*, in French, seemingly unmoved by what was going on. Directly behind her, another woman was very distraught. She was crying into the shoulder of the man seated to her right; he was holding her hand. I heard him say to her, "You've got to calm down." Directly behind that couple sat the man with the goatee. His eyes were fixed on the front bathroom.

I grabbed my son, held my husband's hand, and prayed. The last man came out of the bathroom, and as he passed the man in the yellow shirt he ran his forefinger across his neck and mouthed the word "No."

The plane landed. My husband and I gathered our bags and quickly, very quickly, walked up the jetway. As we entered the airport terminal, I saw a row of men in dark clothing lined up against the wall to the right. Thirty yards out into the terminal, LAPD agents ran past us, heading for the gate. I stopped and looked back. I watched a group of three of the Middle Eastern men stroll off the plane, talking among themselves. The man in the yellow shirt was a few passengers behind the three, walking by himself. An Asian man, who I presumed was an air marshal from the flight, hurried up behind the group of three, flashed a badge, and directed them over to the side.[6] Another man, presumably an air marshal also, approached the man in the yellow shirt, showed him a badge, and directed him to the side.

Later, I learned that representatives of the Federal Bureau of Investigation (FBI), the Los Angeles Police Department (LAPD), the Federal Air Marshal Service (FAMS), the Joint Terrorism Task Force (JTTF) and the Transportation Security Administration (TSA) met our plane as it landed.[7] But not ICE, or Immigration and Customs Enforcement, as it is formally known. ICE is the post-9/11, law enforcement arm of what once was the INS (Immigration and Naturalization Service) and oversees the Federal Air Marshal Service. Most important, ICE agents are responsible for inspecting the documents—passports and visas—of foreigners visiting the United States. I would learn that it is protocol for ICE agents to be present in a situation like flight 327—but they were not.[8]

Seeing what we had seen, my husband and I looked for the person who would be taking statements from passengers. There was no one who appeared to be doing this. We headed to the nearest security agent we could find—away from where flight 327 had landed.

We told airport security that we had been on flight 327 and that we had witnessed many things. Via walkie-talkie,[9] the security guard radioed for assistance, explaining that he had passenger witnesses from flight 327. He asked us to wait. An airport policeman approached us and told us we had to wait while they sorted out "jurisdiction." He gave our son a sticker that looked like a policeman's badge. Another man arrived—I guessed he was an FBI agent, but later I would find out he was a FAM supervisor.[10]

We began to give details, Kevin first. When Kevin started talking about the McDonald's bag, the FAM supervisor interrupted him and used his walkie-talkie to speak to a colleague: "I have a couple here, and they have details about the McDonald's bag." Then he told Kevin to continue, and Kevin stated what he had seen, in great detail.

We listened as the FAM supervisor relayed the information to his colleague, using his walkie-talkie. Based on what the two men said to each other, we understood that

- the man in the yellow shirt told federal agents that he had given the McDonald's bag to the flight attendant;

- the flight attendant told federal agents she had not been given the McDonald's bag by the man in the yellow shirt —or anyone else;

- federal agents found the McDonald's bag in the back of the plane, on the floor underneath the seats.

There was a lot of emphasis on that McDonald's bag.

The FAM supervisor asked Kevin to repeat the specific details of the McDonald's bag, which he did. He then asked Kevin to swear that his information was "100 percent true." Kevin said it was.

The FAM supervisor repeated his question: *Was it 100 percent true?*

Kevin said it was 100 percent true. The FAM supervisor then asked Kevin to hold up his hand and swear the information was true, which he did.

A man came up carrying a handful of passports, opened and stacked flat. They were blue. The FAM supervisor told this second man that we were witnesses and the man with the passports left.

All along, the FAM supervisor had been taking notes on the back of an envelope. He told us he needed more paper and suggested we go to a quieter area. We started walking to a different area of the terminal, when we came upon one of the air marshals from the flight. He was a tall, black man in his thirties.

The FAM supervisor asked the air marshal from the flight if he could borrow some paper. As the marshal hunted through his day planner for paper, I noticed that he had a photograph from an ultrasound scan.

"Are you expecting?" I asked him. He said his wife was pregnant.

We followed the FAM supervisor to a vacant boarding area. He asked us for a few more details. Then he instructed Kevin and me to write statements of what we had seen during the flight. He reminded us to state what we had seen individually, not what we had told each other. I wrote down everything as I remembered it and signed my name at the bottom. The FAM supervisor asked me to raise my right hand and swear that I had "told the truth, the whole truth, and nothing but the truth, so help me God," which I did. Kevin did the same.

Later, when the story became world news, many critics took issue with the number of details I recounted from the flight. How could I remember this or that, with *such specificity*, they asked? The answer is clear: I had written the details down—all of them—immediately after getting off the flight. I had given those specific details to the United States government as evidence of what I considered to be a possible terrorist attempt. And I had sworn to a federal agent that I was telling the truth.

The next day, I combed through the *Los Angeles Times* for news of the incident. There was nothing. I began searching online for news. Again, there was nothing. I asked a friend who is a local news correspondent if there had been any arrests at LAX that day. There hadn't. I called Northwest Airlines' customer service. They said write a letter. I wrote a letter and followed up with a call to their public relations department. They said they were aware of the situation—sorry that happened!—but legally they have thirty days to reply.

I shared my story with a few colleagues. One mentioned that she had been on a flight with a group of foreign men who were acting strangely, but who turned out to be diamond traders. Another had heard a story on National Public Radio (NPR) shortly after 9/11 about a group of Arab musicians who were having a hard time traveling on airplanes throughout the U.S. and couldn't get seats together. I took note of these two stories and began to do a little digging. I came across an article by Jason Burke, a correspondent for the British newspaper, the *Observer* and the author of two books on al-Qaeda, from February 8, 2004:

Terrorist Bid to Build Bombs in Mid-Flight: Intelligence Reveals Dry Runs of New Threat to Blow Up Airliners

Islamic militants have conducted dry runs of a devastating new style of bombing on aircraft flying to Europe, intelligence sources believe.

The tactics, which aim to evade aviation security systems by placing only components of explosive devices on passenger jets, allowing militants to assemble them in the air, have been tried out on planes flying between the Middle East, North Africa and Western Europe, security sources say. . . .

[The] Transportation Security Administration issued an urgent memo detailing new threats to aviation and warning that terrorists in teams of five might be planning suicide missions to hijack commercial airliners, possibly using common items carried by travelers such as cameras, modified as weapons. . . .

An FBI bulletin last November was more specific. It warned that "terrorists are considering the use of improvised explosive devices (IEDS) assembled on board to hijack an aircraft or, alternatively, destroy it over heavily populated areas in the event of passenger or crew resistance.

"Components of IEDS can be smuggled on to an aircraft, concealed in either clothing or personal carry-on items . . . and assembled on board. In many cases of suspicious passenger activity, incidents have taken place in the aircraft's forward lavatory."[11]

According to Burke, the United States government had intelligence from multiple sources that Islamic militants were plotting to blow up airliners by building bombs in aircraft bathrooms. Also according to Burke, the U.S. was aware that terrorists were practicing these tactics overseas by conducting "dry runs." Now terrorists were heading to the United States. On these dry runs, suspicious activity had been taking place in aircraft lavatories.

Burke appeared to be alone in his reporting of the dry runs.[12] But both CNN.com[13] and the *Washington Post*[14] had, the previous summer, reported on the TSA and FBI memos that Burke referred to. The TSA memo,[15] called an "information circular," had gone out to U.S. airlines and law enforcement. It specifically warned that terrorists wanted to hijack commercial airlines "shortly before landing"—thereby eliminating the need for hijacker pilots. The memo also told airlines to closely inspect everyday items that could be disguised weapons, noting, in particular, cameras and shoes.[16]

OPERATION BOJINKA

That terrorists want to build bombs in aircraft bathrooms is not news. The tactic dates from at least 1994, when Ramzi Yousef, along with his uncle, Khalid Sheikh Mohammed (KSM), set out to blow up eleven or twelve U.S. passenger jets over the Pacific Ocean, simultaneously, by building bombs in the aircrafts' bathrooms.[17] The terrorists involved in this plot were not to be suicide bombers. Instead, they would each build a bomb on one leg of each of the eleven or twelve flights, set the bombs' timers for later, and then deplane. If the plan seems overly ambitious, its two masterminds were certainly capable of pulling it off. Ramzi Yousef was the terrorist who tried to bring down the World Trade Center (WTC-1) in 1993 with a truck bomb. Yousef's co-conspirator, KSM, would go on to mastermind the 9/11 attack.

The plot was called Operation Bojinka (*bojinka* is slang in many Arabic dialects for *explosion*[18]), and it was Yousef's next big operation after WTC-1. Yousef had been a kind of one-man terrorist show, barely funded and not very well organized. After his success with WTC-1, that changed. Yousef became respected as an international terrorist. The U.S. government wanted him so badly that they put a $2 million bounty on his head and air-dropped thirty-two thousand matchbooks with Yousef's photo on them in rural Pakistan, hoping to find him.[19] Yousef was able to evade authorities as he traveled extensively throughout Southeast Asia. He was now funded by his wealthy uncle, KSM, as well as his uncle's wealthy business partner, Mohammed Jamal Khalifa—Osama bin Laden's brother-in-law.[20]

For Operation Bojinka, Yousef set about perfecting a small explosive device that could be smuggled onto an aircraft in separate parts—parts disguised as seemingly innocent items. Yousef first tested one of these bombs on December 1, 1994, in the Greenbelt Theatre in Manila. By placing one of his miniature bombs under a theater seat, Yousef simulated the physical conditions he would later face on a plane.[21] The bomb successfully exploded a few hours later. Fortunately, the seat was empty. No one was killed, but a few local theatergoers were hurt.

Yousef worked for another ten days to perfect his bomb. On December 11, he carried out another test for the Bojinka plot, only this time he did it on an actual plane. Posing as an Italian member of parliament—he traveled with a fraudulent Italian passport identifying himself as one "Armaldo Forlani"—Yousef bought a one-way ticket from Manila to Cebu on Philippines Air flight 434.[22] Yousef carried the components of his bomb on him, including nitroglycerin hidden in a bottle of contact lens solution and bomb stabilizers disguised as cotton balls. In the hollowed-out heels of his shoes, Yousef hid batteries.[23]

During the flight, Yousef asked the flight attendant if he could change seats, saying he needed a better view. In truth, he wanted to occupy a seat over the plane's fuselage near the exit door.[24] Half-way through the flight, Yousef assembled the bomb in the aircraft's bathroom. Returning to his seat, he placed the bomb inside the life vest underneath. He set the timer for several hours later and deplaned.

On the next leg of the flight, the bomb exploded. The twenty-three-year-old Japanese businessman, Haruki Ike-gami, who was sitting where Yousef had sat, died a miserable death, his legs separated from the rest of his body. Fortu-nately for the 273 other passengers and twenty flight crew on board the 747, the captain made a heroic, emergency landing on nearby Okinawa Island.[25] The bomb was too small to destroy the plane in mid-air, and Yousef set about fine-tuning his calculations.

A few weeks later, shortly before Operation Bojinka was set to unveil, Yousef was building bombs in his Manila apart-ment, when one of them exploded. A fire started and Yousef fled. Manila police discovered a cache of information about the terrorist on his computer, which interrupted Bojinka. Had the plot succeeded, it's likely that four thousand civilians would have been killed. Some of the details are extraordi-nary: Yousef needed his bombs to explode in seats above the planes' central fuel tanks, adjacent to the wings. When the bombs went off, they would ignite the plane's fuel, causing a massive, secondary explosion.[26] Investigators would also learn that Yousef wanted the bombs to explode over heavily populated areas of the United States.[27]

In his *Observer* article from February 2004, Jason Burke reported that terrorists were again working on the nightmare scenario of building bombs in aircraft bathrooms. Burke detailed a 2002 incident in which a Moroccan jet landing in Metz, France, was found to have one hundred grams of pentrite (the explosive used by shoe-bomber Richard Reid) hidden in an armrest. French officials believed the explosives were placed on the jet in a "trial run." At the time of the article, such incidents had only amounted to dry runs. In August 2004 that changed. The Bojinka scenario became real.

On the night of August 24, 2004, two civilian aircraft in Russia exploded, almost simultaneously, killing all ninety passengers and crew. The mid-air explosions were caused by terrorists' bombs. The events were widely reported and has since been confirmed by the U.S. Department of State.[28]

Not as widely reported was that Russian investigators believe the detonations occurred in the two planes' toilets. According to the Russian newspaper *Gazeta*, "At first, the experts on explosives were puzzled as they saw no traces of explosions in the passenger salons or noses of the planes. However, when the tail part of the TU-154 was examined, in the area where the toilet is, a piece of the edging with the illuminator had been torn away."[29]

Pravda.Ru, one of Russia's leading sources for news online, ran an article which was headlined: "TU-134 and TU-154 Were Exploded From Their Toilets." The article explains that investigators concluded, "martyrs put the explosives in action in the toilets. For this reason, there was no fire on the planes and most of the bodies were neither burned nor disfigured by the explosion."[30]

Further supporting this theory, Voice of America (an international broadcasting service with a weekly audience of ninety-six million people) reported that "the body parts of one woman were scattered widely on the ground. Officials said parts of her legs were found in the toilet section of one plane, leading to speculation that she might have detonated some kind of explosive from there."[31]

The attacks were carried out by two female suicide bombers. Both women have been linked to Chechen terrorists. Meanwhile, a radical Islamic group called the "Islambouli Brigades of al-Qaeda" immediately stepped forward to claim responsibility for both crashes.[32] Within hours of the crash, the Islamic group claimed it had five people, or "mujahadeen," on board each aircraft, stating, "There will be, God willing, more waves until we humiliate the infidel state called Russia."[33]

One week after the dual plane explosions, two more female suicide bombers blew themselves up, this time in a subway north of Moscow. Ten people were killed and another fifty-one were injured. These two women had shared an apartment with the two suicide bombers from the plane attacks; two were sisters. The explosive Hexogen was used in all three attacks, which the State Department calls a "safe and inexpensive explosive." The State Department believes the attacks were "well planned," adding that, "terrorists conducted significant pre-operational surveillance."[34]

The following day, on September 1, 2004, between seventeen and thirty-five masked men and women seized a middle school in the Russian town of Beslan, taking over one thousand civilian hostages. Three hundred and forty-four civilians were killed, and at least 172 of them children. Hundreds more were wounded and terrorized. The siege occurred on a popular Russian holiday, "First September," also known as the "Day of Knowledge." Parents and grandparents accompany their children to school to celebrate learning. It is believed that the terrorists involved in the Beslan School Seige specifically chose this remarkable day for the devastating effect it would have on entire families.[35]

Chechen terrorists and fundamentalist Islamic extremists have joined forces, and they appear to have done so with the help of "the most wanted man in Russia," Chechen warlord Shamil Basayev. Shortly after the Beslan School Seige, Basayev claimed responsibility for all the attacks.[36] He praised different factions of various terror organization for different elements of the attacks, but made it clear the groups were all united in the same cause, "killing and humiliating infidels."[37]

Chechens are a largely Muslim ethnic group who have lived for centuries in the mountainous Caucasus region, located south of Moscow and north of Iran. The area has been ravaged by conflict since 1994, with at least one hundred thousand civilians and ten thousand Russian troops killed in the fighting. Support for the Chechen cause is widespread throughout the Arab world, and the Arab news network Al-Jazeera frequently broadcasts reports of Russian abuses against Muslims there.[38]

To date, Arab commanders are leading the majority of rebel forces in Chechnya—fighting in the name of jihad, or holy war. What began a decade ago as largely hit-and-miss attacks against the Russian army (Chechnya wants autonomy from Russia) has now progressed to the widespread use of terror.

Whether the Islambouli Brigades of al-Qaeda is directly linked to Osama bin Laden is not yet clear, but the terrorists' affiliation with bin Laden's al-Qaeda—and indirectly with Ramzi Yousef of Operation Bojinka—cannot be overlooked.[39] The group's late, eponymous leader, Lt. Khaled Islambouli, killed Egyptian president Anwar Sadat during a military parade in Cairo in 1981. Islambouli was executed for the crime a year later. He was a member of the terrorist organization Egyptian Islamic Jihad, and was inspired to kill Sadat by the preachings of the Blind Sheikh, Omar Abdel Rahman, the terrorist who is presently serving a life sentence in a U.S. prison for his involvement in the first bombing of the World Trade Center in 1993 (among other bomb plots)—alongside Ramzi Yousef. According to the *9/11 Commission Report*,Egyptian Islamic Jihad merged its organization with bin Laden's al-Qaeda in the late 1990s.[40]

Female suicide bombers (also called "black widows") with links to Islamic fundamentalists are on the rise. Their effectiveness in committing terror attacks in Russia is daunting. The State Department notes, "social customs preclude male security guards from thoroughly searching Muslim women."[41] In 2002, a crowded Moscow theater was taken over by fifty Chechen rebels—eighteen of them women dressed in black and strapped with explosive belts. Shamil

Basayev also claimed responsibility for planning this raid and, specifically, for training the women for jihad.

As early as 2001, *Pravda* reported that Arab mercenaries were training female suicide bombers in training camps that had been set up in the Chechen mountains. The women were being trained "by Arab instructors from Khattab's gang" to carry out suicide attacks.[42]

Khattab is the late Chechen warlord who appeared on a 2002 fundraising videotape with Osama bin Laden (the two men fought side by side against the Soviet Union as mujahadeen in Afghanistan throughout the 1980s). The videotape inter-cuts scenes of terrorist activities in al-Qaeda training camps in Afghanistan with those on the Chechen battlefields. Also on the tape, alongside Khattab, is Shamil Basayev. The videotape was purchased by the newspaper *Newsday* from a landlord in Kabul, who claimed his tenants, al-Qaeda members, fled during the U.S. bombing and left the tape behind.[43]

While Muslim jihadis are lining up to die, where they go, and which conflicts they enter into, doesn't necessarily matter to them. Or, as stated in the *9/11 Commission Report*, it's decided *for* them. Mohammad Atta, the ringleader of the 9/11 hijacking plot, initially planned to join the fight in Chechnya. Bin Laden, however, had a different assignment for Atta. Zacarias Moussaoui was reported to have been a recruiter for al-Qaeda–backed rebels in Chechnya—before he took up flight training in America and joined the 9/11 plot.[44] Moussaoui is the only person in the United States to have been charged in connection with the 9/11 attacks. He pled guilty in April 2005.

—

If the idea of bombs in aircraft bathrooms isn't news, neither is the idea of terrorist test flights, or "surveillance flights," as they are called in the *9/11 Commission Report*. The 9/11 hijackers took dozens of these surveillance flights before they flew their final missions, studying factors that were constant and would not change on the day they actually took over the aircraft. This included a plane's layout (seating, aisles, and locations of lavatories and galleys) and the in-flight procedures of a flight crew.[45] To study the specifics of these non-variables, the hijackers were reported to have videotaped flight crews and, in one instance, gotten a tour of the cockpit.[46] Sometimes these surveillance flights are called "dry runs."[47]

New to counterterrorism vernacular is the idea of a "probe." Probe is the term used inside the Federal Air Marshal Service to describe "operatives gathering intelligence"[48] about what goes on during commercial airline flights. A probe is inherently different than a surveillance flight because it involves testing non-variables, that is, testing a human being's response or the response of a group. The meaning of a probe is simplified in the words of one air marshal that I interviewed: "The word *probe*? Think *poke*.

Imagine someone poking you. They poke you in the leg, you respond one way. They poke you in the arm, you respond a different way. Then they poke you in the ribs and you respond a different way altogether. They keep poking you, sometimes lightly; other pokes are like a jab. They're paying attention to exactly what *you* do in response to their pokes. That's the whole point of a probe, to push the system. They're going to poke you everywhere but in the eyes."[49]

Before 9/11, flight attendants and commercial airline pilots received training that taught them to cooperate with hijackers. Before 9/11, statistics indicated that the longer a flight crew cooperated with hijackers, the more likely it was the conflict would end without casualties. Before 9/11, how passengers reacted to hijackers was largely a non-variable; the majority of passengers did as they were told. The small minority who didn't were the ones most likely to be killed.[50]

Because of the events on United flight 93 (the flight that crashed into a Pennsylvania field on 9/11), terrorists now know that passengers and flight crew can and will fight back. If a U.S. passenger plane is going to be hijacked any time in the future, hijackers will have new variables to deal with: passengers, flight crew, and federal air marshals. How will the passengers and flight crew react? How will the air marshals respond to certain events as they unfold? To answer these questions, would-be terrorists have to gather intelligence on passenger, flight crew, and air marshal reactions to various situations. They do this through probes.

FLYING WHILE ARAB

Prior to flight 327, the U.S. government had issued dual warnings, one through the TSA and another through the FBI, that law enforcement should be wary of groups of five men on a plane who might be trying to build bombs in the bathroom. With this in mind, shouldn't a group of fourteen Middle Eastern men from a terrorist-sponsoring nation have been individually screened before boarding a domestic U.S. flight?[51]

Apparently not. According to our own rules against discrimination, it can't be done. During the 9/11 hearings, 9/11 commissioner John Lehman stated that "it was the policy (before 9/11) and I believe remains the policy today to fine airlines if they have more than two young Arab males in secondary questioning because that's discriminatory."[52] So even if Northwest Airlines personnel had searched two of the men before they boarded the flight, they couldn't have searched the other twelve because they would have already filled a government-imposed quota.

In her column, "Arab Hijackers Now Eligible For Pre-Boarding," columnist Ann Coulter observed that only ten days after 9/11, Secretary of Transportation Norman Mineta faxed a letter to all U.S. airlines, reminding the airlines that it is illegal to discriminate against passengers based on their race, color, national or ethnic origin, or religion. Coulter noted that Mineta's letter also, and unflinchingly, was faxed to American Airlines and United Airlines—carriers who together had lost eight pilots, twenty-five flight attendants, and two-hundred and thirteen passengers to Arab hijackers just a few days before.[53]

A few months after sending the letter, at Mr. Mineta's behest, the Department of Transportation (DOT) filed complaints against United Airlines and American Airlines for just such discrimination. In November 2003, United Airlines settled their case with the DOT for $1.5 million. In March 2004, American Airlines settled their case with the DOT for $1.5 million. The DOT also charged Continental Airlines with discriminating against passengers who appeared to be Arab, Middle Eastern, or Muslim. Continental Airlines settled their complaint with the DOT in April 2004 for $500,000.[54] In June 2002, the American Civil Liberties Union (ACLU) and the American-Arab Anti-Discrimination Committee launched a series of lawsuits over cases of men being removed from airplanes. These cases became known as "Flying While Arab." By May 2005, several of these cases had been settled for an "undisclosed amount."[55]

It seems the airlines are working hard to avoid further suits. One flight attendant informed me that it is her airline's policy not to refer to people as "Middle Eastern men." Political correctness has become a roadblock for airline safety. I've learned from my many emails and interviews with airline personnel that the airlines' fear of being accused of racial profiling could very well lead to another 9/11.

From what I witnessed, Northwest Airlines doesn't have to worry about Norman Mineta's filing a complaint against it for discriminatory secondary screening of Arab men. No one checked the passports of the Syrian men to match the people with their identification. No one inspected the contents of the two instrument cases or the McDonald's bag. And no one checked the limping man's orthopedic shoe. In fact, according to TSA regulations, passengers wearing orthopedic shoes won't be asked to take them off. As the TSA website states, "Advise the screener if you're wearing orthopedic shoes . . . screeners should not be asking you to remove your orthopedic shoes at any time during the screening process."[56]

No one checked our identification. No one checked the folds in my newspaper or the contents of my son's backpack. No one asked us what we had done during our layover, if we had bought anything, or if anyone gave us anything. We were asked all of these questions (and many others) three weeks earlier when we had traveled in Europe—where passengers with airport layovers are rigorously questioned and screened before boarding any flight. In Detroit, no one checked who we were or what we carried on board a 757 jetliner bound for America's second-most-populated city.

I placed a call to the TSA and talked to Joe Dove, a customer service supervisor. I told him how my family and I had eaten with metal utensils in an airport diner moments before boarding the flight and that no one checked our luggage or the instrument cases carried on board by the Middle Eastern men. Dove's response was, "Restaurants in secured areas—that's an ongoing problem. We get that complaint often. TSA gets that complaint all the time, and they haven't worked that out with the FAA. They're aware of it. You've got a good question. There may not be a reasonable answer at this time. I'm not going to BS you."[57]

Rafi Ron is an authority on and an advocate of passenger profiling. As the former head of security at Israel's Ben Gurion Airport, he is an expert on the subject. What Ron told Congress, in February 2002, about passenger profiling is fascinating.[58] After an El Al flight was hijacked by Palestinian and Syrian terrorists in 1968, the Israeli government determined that a real threat existed and a system needed to be put in place to combat that threat. They also determined that a thorough passenger check amounted to a fifty-seven minute procedure. An hour search per person, in any airport, in any country, would be far too time-consuming (not to mention expensive), so the Israeli government put a *passenger* profiling system in place—not a *racial* profiling system, a *passenger* profiling one.

El Al uses a method that allows airport personnel to make intelligent decisions—not racist decisions—about who might be a good candidate for a more thorough search. It's hard to argue that the El Al system doesn't work: the airline hasn't lost a plane to terrorists in over thirty-five years. Terrorists certainly haven't lost interest in Israeli aviation, they've simply been stymied.

It has been argued that people, not machines, are better equipped to thwart terror attacks, and El Al's passenger profiling system is a terrific example of this. In 1986, El Al agents at Ben Gurion Airport discovered a bomb *before* it got on board a plane. No machine has ever done that. I'm referring to the infamous case of the pregnant Irish girl, Ann Marry Murphy, who was profiled by El Al agents. Factors that led to her profiling remain classified, but it is on the record that agents learned that Ms. Murphy's Palestinian boyfriend (and the father of her child) had packed her bag but was not traveling with her. A more extensive search of her carry-on bag revealed seven pounds of Cemtex (an explosive) sewn into its lining, as well as a sophisticated timing device disguised as a calculator.

Ms. Murphy's case illustrates why El Al does not call its profiling system a "racial" system. So does the more recent case of El Al agents' successful profiling of "shoe-bomber" Richard Reid. Reid took an El Al flight a few months before he took the American Airlines flight we now know he tried to blow up with explosives hidden in his shoe. El Al employees at the Amsterdam airport profiled Reid—a Muslim convert of Jamaican and English heritage—and found him suspicious. Again, the profiling factors remain secret, but we certainly know Reid wasn't being tapped for what the ACLU calls "Flying While Arab"—he isn't an Arab. A head-to-heel search revealed nothing illegal on Reid, but El Al security felt uncomfortable enough about his behavior that they seated an air marshal next to him during his flight to Tel Aviv. This occurred before 9/11.

Five months later, in December 2001, American Airlines agents in Paris, France, also felt Reid was suspicious: he paid for his one-way ticket to Miami, Florida, with cash, and he carried nothing but a Koran in an otherwise empty backpack. That day was also the anniversary of the downing of the Pan Am flight over Lockerbie, Scotland, in 1988. After detaining Reid and finding nothing illegal on him, American Airlines paid for his hotel room and allowed him to take the next flight to Miami—the one he tried to blow up. Too bad American Airlines didn't take a page out of El Al's playbook and seat an air marshal next to Reid. As we now know, the 197 passengers on board had an extremely narrow miss.

Other testimony at the same aviation security hearing at which Ron testified (on the constitutionality of passenger profiling) came from Jonathan Turley, a professor at Georgetown who has taught, written, and litigated about constitutional law for over a decade. Turley argued for what he calls "airport profiling."

Turley used the example of police profiling African Americans for drug busts in the inner cities as an example of racial profiling. But like Rafi Ron, Turley reminded Congress that when it comes to profiling in airports, we're not talking about *racial* profiling, we're talking about *passenger* profiling. "Society can live with a couple of nickel bags of narcotics making it through the law enforcement net," Turley said, but added that the costs of a terrorist making it though airport security net is "far more immediate and deadly." Turley closed with a powerful statement, that "failures at airports' security are not measured by nickel bags but body bags." This, he said, is a reality that cannot be ignored.[59]

Two days after my experience on Northwest 327 came this notice: "The U.S. Transportation Security Administration has issued a new directive which demands pilots make a pre-flight announcement banning passengers from congregating in aisles and outside the plane's toilets. The directive also orders flight attendants to check the toilets every two hours for suspicious packages."[60]

It's unlikely that that TSA issued this report based on the events on Northwest 327—they would have had only two days to do so. It is more likely that the TSA was, after many months, finally responding to overseas intelligence reports that terrorists had been conducting dry runs and were now heading to America.

SCRUBBED

A few days after my flight, I was at a regular staff meeting at WomensWallStreet.com, when I told my colleagues about the flight. The webzine's editor in chief, Pamela Little, said that I must write about the incident. The editorial staff debated whether it was something that WomensWallStreet should publish, or whether we would first try to get a bigger paper involved. As a team, we decided on the latter. After an introduction by the webzine's public relations firm, Porter Novelli, a terrorism reporter for the *Washington Post* contacted me.

I talked briefly with the journalist about my experience. He immediately asked if I had any other witness' information aside from my husband's. He called the story a "one-source" story and said he would get back to me. He never did, but within a few hours, I received a rather surprising call. Dave Adams introduced himself as the Federal Air Marshal Service's head of public affairs. Adams told me that he had spoken with the reporter from the *Post* and that he had heard I was considering writing a story about the flight. He wanted to assure me that there was nothing nefarious about the Middle Eastern men, that they were "just musicians." Adams told me he wanted to clear a few things up. We spoke for almost an hour.

Adams explained that the Middle Eastern men on flight 327 were Syrians. He told me they were questioned, individually and at length, by the FAMS, the FBI, and the TSA—at the airport. He explained that "it all checked out," that the fourteen Syrians had been hired as musicians to play at a casino in the desert. Adams said they were "scrubbed." None had arrest records (in America, I presume), none showed up on the FBI's "no fly" list or its Most Wanted Terrorists List. It was as simple as that, he said. The men checked out, and they were let go. According to Adams, the fourteen men traveled on Northwest Airlines flight 327 using one-way tickets. A few days later they flew from Long Beach, California, to New York City on JetBlue—also using one-way tickets. I wondered why Adams told me about the tickets, it seemed one-way tickets for fourteen men would be incredibly cost-prohibitive for a Syrian band. I asked Adams what kind of instruments the men played. Adams said that "they didn't get that far into the weeds." I asked what that meant. Adams said that the agents hadn't checked the instruments—what they were or even if the men had any.

I asked Adams why, based on the FBI's credible information that terrorists may try to assemble bombs on planes, the air marshals or the flight attendants didn't do anything about the men's bizarre behavior, specifically the frequent trips to the lavatories. "Our FAM agents have to have an event to arrest somebody," Adams explained. "Our agents aren't going to deploy until there is an actual event." Adams said he couldn't speak for the policies of Northwest Airlines.[61]

What I didn't know then, but was later reported by James Langton in the London *Telegraph*, was that on the same day as my flight, "only hours earlier, the Department of Homeland Security had issued an urgent alert at half a dozen airports for a group of six Pakistani men believed to be training for a terrorist attack in the US."[62] Two of those airports, Langton noted, were Detroit and Los Angeles.

I didn't buy what Adams told me, that nothing nefarious had happened on flight 327. I couldn't fathom why the men had been interviewed and let go. I wrote a story for WomensWallStreet.com, under the headline, "Terror in the Skies, Again?" In that article, I detailed what I had seen, and I explained what I had learned. And I ended the piece with these questions: Were these men really *just musicians*? If nineteen terrorists can learn to fly airplanes, couldn't fourteen terrorists learn to play instruments? Soon a great many others would be asking these questions as well.

2

Landing on Capitol Hill

WOMENSWALLSTREET.COM (WWS) published my account of flight 327 on Tuesday, July 13, 2004. A notice about the article was included in the webzine's *Daily Cents* email, a subscriber newsletter which usually features financial tips for women. By the next morning, WWS page views were unusually high, on the order of ten times the normal number. Apparently our readers had been emailing the article to their friends, family, and colleagues, and everyone was reading it. By Thursday morning, the number of page views had again multiplied ten-fold; more than a half a million readers had visited the site.[1]

That this first article became world news and led to a Congressional investigation owes, in part, to the existence of the *blogosphere*, that is, the world of "blogs." Blog is short for weblog, a webpage that offers the opinion of its author (the blogger) on all kinds of things from the personal to the political. If you've never heard of or visited a blog, you're not alone. According to a Pew internet study, in November 2004, 62 percent of Internet users didn't know what a blog was.[2] In July 2004 that 62 percent included me.

Blogs are a relatively new Internet phenomenon. In 1999, there were only some fifty blogs.[3] But five years later, when the first article in the "Terror in The Skies, Again?" series was published, there were nearly eight million of them. A year after that, on the day in June 2005 that I wrote this chapter, there were 11,265,249 blogs with 1,206,189,351 links.[4] And counting.

According to two political scientists, Daniel Drezner (himself a blogger) and Henry Farrell, out of the many millions of blogs, a few stand out. They call them the *elite* blogs—blogs that the mainstream media read and take seriously. If any of the so-called elite blogs finds a story interesting, no matter how small or underreported that story may be, their attention makes it into a bigger story.[5] And that is exactly what happened with "Terror in the Skies, Again?" In "Web of Influence," published in the November-December 2004 issue of *Foreign Policy*, Drezner and Farrell explain:

> The blogosphere also acts as a barometer for whether a story would or should receive greater coverage by the mainstream media. The more blogs that discuss a particular issue, the more likely that the blogosphere will set the agenda for future news coverage. Consider one recent example with regard to Homeland Security. In July 2004, Annie Jacobsen, a writer for

WomensWallStreet.com, posted online a first-person account of suspicious activity by Syrian passengers on a domestic U.S. flight....

Her account was quickly picked up, linked to, and vigorously debated throughout the blogosphere.... In just one weekend, 2 million people read her article. Reports soon followed in the mainstream media outlets such as NPR, MSNBC, *Time* and the *New York Times*, prompting a broader national debate about the racial profiling of possible terrorists.[6]

In other words, when certain bloggers say something is important, it becomes important to other bloggers, and the story spreads across the Internet among bloggers. In certain cases, as in mine, a story spreads like wildfire, consuming the interest not just of bloggers themselves, but also of their friends and family, who in turn email the story to their friends, family, neighbors, and colleagues. When this happens, a story reaches critical mass.

Different bloggers focused on different elements of "Terror in The Skies, Again?" Glenn Reynolds, whose blog, Instapundit.com, is considered by many to be an elite blog, drew parallels between flight 327 and the James Woods incident the month *before* 9/11. I wasn't familiar with the Woods incident and was surprised to learn about it.

On August 1, 2001, the actor flew on an American Airlines flight from Boston to Los Angeles. Alarmed by the behavior of a group of four Middle Eastern men, Woods summoned the pilot (this was back in the days when pilots came out of the cockpit to speak with concerned passengers). He discreetly pointed to the four men he was talking about and told the pilot, "I think they're going to hijack this plane."[7] The pilot assured Woods that the cockpit door would remain locked for the remainder of the trip. A report was filed with the FAA on Woods's behalf but, tragically, no one followed up with Woods or the men. The day after 9/11, several federal agents showed up in Woods' kitchen at 7:15 in the morning. They wanted to talk about the flight.

In June 2002, Woods told Seymour M. Hersh of the *New Yorker* that he was so uncomfortable about the men's behavior that he hung onto his (then metal) cutlery after dinner. "They were in synch," he told Hersh. Hersh tried to verify Woods's story with the FBI and was told by a senior official, "the bureau had subsequently investigated Woods's story but had not been able to find evidence of the hijackers on the flight Woods thought he had taken." Then the official added, "We don't know for sure."[8]

On another elite blog, TheBleat.com, James Lileks wondered what would happen if a terrorist attack like the Bojinka plot were to happen today. "I tell you," Lileks observed, "something like this happens on a big scale—lots of planes dropping out of the sky, half the country is going to ask for detention camps. All because we didn't dare delay or inconvenience self-professed bands of Syrian 'musicians' because it might suggest we were (gasp) dispositionally suspicious of a dozen Syrians clutching violin cases. Is profiling a good idea? Read the piece, put yourself on that plane before you answer the question."[9]

LittleGreenFootballs.com was alarmed by the sheer number of Syrians on my flight and pushed one theory about terrorists using larger hijacking teams to take over planes. "What if passengers are faced with a highly organized team of 15-20 hijackers, with unconventional and undetectable weapons, conditioned by a lifetime of indoctrination to commit mind-wrenchingly savage acts of violence?" one blogger on the site wrote. "And what if our government is still too hobbled by political correctness to recognize threats in time to deal with them—before the hijackers board the plane?"[10] A horrifying thought, indeed.

Michelle Malkin, a syndicated columnist and best-selling author who blogs at MichelleMalkin.com, put on her reporter's cap and went after the facts. She spoke to Dave Adams of the FAMS and confirmed the basic facts laid out in my article. Adams told Malkin that he was quoted accurately in my story.

While the elite bloggers discussed the story among themselves, their readers (by posting comments) debated whether the story was a hoax, whether I really exist, and what they would have done if they had been on that plane. Other bloggers spit tacks. To many, I was a racist, paranoid xenophobe, a hysterical housewife, and a sniveling little twit. For every blogger that leaped to my defense, another joined a cyber-group called "People Against Annie Jacobsen."

Bloggers posted updates on flight 327 for weeks, defending their previous posts and hyperlinking to other bloggers whose updates supported theirs. Everyone, it seemed, had a pony in the race.

Many people's reaction to the story went far beyond the story itself. "Terror in The Skies, Again?" became a measure of how people have coped with their own feelings, particularly about Muslims and terrorism after 9/11, feelings they couldn't or wouldn't otherwise express. Many who read the story instantly moved into one of two camps, for or against. You were either a Montague or a Capulet; you were a Hatfield or a McCoy.

Meanwhile, another type of discussion was also taking place on other blogs, one that cut to a most disturbing heart of the matter: With the War on Terror going on, what would become of relationships between certain peoples? Between Christians and Muslims, between Americans and the rest of the world. One side shouted that Americans like me had become so blinded by "Islamophobia and religious bigotry" that we were beyond reason, driven literally insane by fear. The other side suggested that those who opposed Annie Jacobsen should go back to the wonderfully open societies they came from, "places like Saudi Arabia or Iran."

On the fourth day, the story caught the attention of the *Wall Street Journal.* Online editor James Taranto recommended the article, calling it the best read on the Web that day. Taranto picked up on the absurd and disturbing paradox I presented in the article: that (a) American intelligence agencies fear that terrorists aim to build bombs in aircraft bathrooms, and yet (b) federal air marshals, seated on U.S. commercial aircraft to prevent the next terror attack, won't deploy unless an actual "event" takes place.

Drezner and Farrell were right about the power of blogs. In less than a week, WomensWallStreet.com had more than three million visitors,[11] which doesn't count how many times the story was emailed.

That my article became world news also owes largely to the power of email. Within a few weeks, the article had been read by millions of people around the globe. It had been reprinted in South Africa and Turkey and translated into German, Arabic, and Chinese. All because people had been referred to it by someone they trusted—via an email.

Pulitzer Prize–winning author and *New York Times* columnist Thomas L. Friedman hit the nail on the head when he wrote about just how powerful email can be: "Jody Williams won the Nobel Prize in 1997 for helping to build an international coalition to bring a treaty outlawing land mines. Although nearly 120 governments endorsed the treaty, it was opposed by Russia, China, and the United States. When Jody Williams was asked, 'How did you do that? How did you organize one thousand different citizens' groups and nongovernmental organizations on five continents to forge a treaty that was opposed by the major powers?' she had a very brief answer. 'E-mail.'"[12]

In those first few days after "Terror in The Skies, Again?" was published, I received more than five thousand emails at the WomensWallStreet.com headquarters. The majority supported my efforts; a few said things unfit to print. One email was a death threat. A United States senator offered legal help, pro bono, if I ever needed it; one octogenarian grandmother told me to never let up.

What surprised me most were the more than two hundred emails I received from commercial pilots, flight attendants, and other airline employees, many of whom are contractually forbidden to speak with the press about "accidents and incidents," but who wrote to me anyway because they had something important to say. Those who could go on the record, did.

Gary Boettcher, a pilot for American Airlines who is now president of the Coalition of Allied Pilots Associations,[13] a group that represents twenty-two thousand professional pilots, wrote, "Folks, I am a Captain with a major airline. I was very involved with the Arming Pilots effort. Your reprint of this airborne event is not a singular nor isolated experience. The terrorists are probing us all the time."[14]

Later, Boettcher told me that, based on his experience, it was his opinion that I was likely on a dry run. He has had many of these experiences, and so have many of his fellow captains. They have been trying to speak out about this, but so far their words have been falling on deaf ears.

Mark Bogosian, B-757/767 pilot for American Airlines, wrote, "the incident you wrote about, and incidents like it, occur more than you like to think. It is a 'dirty little secret' that all of us, as crew members, have known about for quite some time."[15] Rand Peck, a captain for a major U.S. airline, wrote me to say,

> I'm deeply bothered by the inconsistencies that I observe at TSA. I've observed matronly looking grandmothers, practically disrobed at security check points and five-year-old blonde boys turned inside out, while Middle Eastern males sail through undetained. We have little to fear from grandmothers and little boys. But Middle Eastern males are protected, not by our Constitution, but from our current popular policy of political correctness and a desire to offend no one at any cost, regardless of how many airplanes and bodies litter the landscape. This is my personal opinion, formed by my experiences and observations.[16]

Thomas Heidenberger, a pilot for a major U.S. airline, contacted me, and I interviewed him at length. His wife, Michele, was the senior flight attendant aboard American Airlines flight 77, which was hijacked and crashed into the Pentagon. "Keep writing, Annie, don't give up," Captain Heidenberger told me one of the times I spoke to him. "I've been walking the long halls of Congress and I can't do it any more. I have a family to support," he told me another time. "You've gotten national attention. Do something good with it." And then he said this, which I'll never forget: "The airlines still aren't as safe as they could be, and my kids can't afford to lose another parent."

What really surprised me was the overwhelming support I immediately received from flight attendants.[17] In my first article, I did not paint the flight attendants on flight 327 in the most glowing light. In fact, I made it clear that I felt they didn't do an important part of their job: to insist that the Syrians sit down—certainly when the plane was landing.[18]

An explanation for this came by way of Jeanne M. Elliott, security coordinator for the Professional Flight Attendants Association (PFAA), which represents the flight attendants of Northwest Airlines among others. Ms. Elliott wrote, "By the uneducated eye, and to those who don't walk in our shoes, it may have been perceived that we were doing nothing, when indeed we were putting the safety and security of those passengers as our first priority." Later, Ms. Elliot explained this further, saying that "the things flight attendants needed to adequately perform aviation security functions have been delayed and/or ignored."[19] At the top of this list of needs, Elliott noted, is appropriate training.

Particularly interesting were the emails that came from government sources—some anonymous, some not—all letting me know that they had read the article and that it had gotten the attention of some in the United States government. In many cases, at the head or tail of those emails were long lists of other email addresses ending in ".gov." In other words, the article or its link had been sent, via email, to hundreds of government officials who, in turn, emailed the article to colleagues they felt should read it.

This is how I came to know that one of the government's bomb-making experts and scientific advisors for the TSA had read the article. In turn, he sent "Terror in The Skies, Again?" to dozens of his colleagues. I left several messages for this individual, but he never returned my call.

There was one email I kept handy when, in the weeks to come, the going got rough. It was from a woman working in the Department of Homeland Security (DHS). I won't give her name, though she had the chutzpah to sign her name to her email—and this at a time when nary a DHS agent would return my phone calls.[20] She wrote: "I picked up the initial story and circulated it among our group (General Aviation); I also sent it to a friend at the White House and NORAD. It was read very widely on this end, and those who should take notice, believe me, took notice. It was a great article."

INTO THE WEEDS

NBC was the first major news outlet to contact Womens-WallStreet.com. The producer I spoke with said the FBI had confirmed that fourteen Syrians were on the flight. She said the FBI confirmed the details of what happened upon landing in Los Angeles. The accounts from the flight attendants regarding what happened during the flight, the FBI said, matched the accounts given by me and my husband.[21]

Next, I spoke with a producer from ABC. She explained that she could not get Dave Adams, head of public affairs for the FAMS, on the phone. So she asked me some of the questions that she had wanted to ask him: Where exactly did this band of fourteen musicians play? What was the name of the band? Who booked the band, and what kind of music did they play? Did anyone follow up and actually witness these fourteen men performing at their desert casino gig? I had none of the answers, even though I had asked Adams these exact questions myself when we had spoken the week before. The ABC producer also asked me other questions which had crossed my mind after hanging up with Adams: Did I know anything about their return flight on JetBlue? Did the men go back to Syria? Did I believe the FAMS story?

I wrote a second article on flight 327. That night, July 19, 2004, Kevin and I appeared on MSNBC's *Scarborough Country* with Joe Scarborough. At this point, the FAMS was confirming the facts of flight 327—that the pilot radioed ahead for back-up because there were fourteen Syrian musicians on board who, "regrettably," were acting suspiciously. Where the FAMS and I differed was in our interpretation of what the Syrians were up to. I felt something nefarious was happening; the FAMS asserted their behavior was innocent.

After Scarborough talked with Kevin and me about the flight, experts were brought on to debate what we had said. Steve Pomerantz, former FBI chief of counterterrorism, was one of them. He immediately contested my assertion that flight 327 was a dry run and made this bold statement:

> I'm struck by a couple of things. One is, or course, that nothing happened. We can talk about suspicious

behavior. We can talk about all these activities, but the
bottom line is, nothing occurred on that flight.

The FBI [conducted] a very thorough, exhaustive
investigation during the course of which nobody was
charged with a crime. Nobody was even detained,
which tells me the people were here legally, legitimately,
had official and appropriate documentation.[22]

Pomerantz is a "former" agent, and I wondered how he
could claim to know anything about this specific incident
since he was no longer employed by the FBI. But as a former FBI agent, one would assume he knew the definition of
thorough, and I asked him about this at the end of the show.
"Joe, I have one question," I said, "and it's off the former FBI
director's comment that a thorough investigation had been
done. I would like to know what 'thorough' is because I asked
Dave [Adams] what kind of instruments they had. And he
told me that they 'hadn't gotten that far into the weeds.'"[23]

Scarborough Country was out of time, and Pomerantz
wasn't given an opportunity to respond. Lucky for him.
Anything he said would have revealed that he had absolutely
no idea just how *un*-thorough the investigation of flight 327
had been. That the FAMs hadn't checked the Syrians' instruments was a small detail compared to the facts that would
eventually come out. The FAMs and the FBI had interviewed
only two of the Syrians—not all fourteen as they would
repeatedly insist to various news organizations. And the
interviews lasted for ten or fifteen minutes, not the "probably almost two hours" they had been telling reporters.[24]

Pomerantz's three main assertions—that nothing happened, that the FBI conducted an exhaustive investigation, and that the Syrians were on the flight legally ("in status")—would later all be proved wrong.

The public didn't buy what Pomerantz, was saying. His approach—*assume the government is doing its job*—is something from a bygone era. People watching the show literally flooded Scarborough with (again) emails. On air, Joe expressed how surprised even he was by the sheer number of them. And that got Joe Scarborough digging.

Three days later, on July 22, 2004, the *9/11 Commission Report* was released. Its findings were all over the news. "The United States government was simply not active enough in combating the terrorist threat before 9/11," announced the commission's chairman, Thomas Kean. One of the key findings of the report was that, leading up to 9/11, various government agencies (the FBI, CIA, and INS in particular) were not working together and, because of this, glaring opportunities to catch the hijackers had been missed.

That night, Joe Scarborough again headlined flight 327 on his show, interviewing NBC investigative reporter Scott Weinberger. Weinberger had uncovered a major failure in the flight 327 investigation: the Syrians' visas were expired.

> SCARBOROUGH: We've been discussing Northwest flight 327 all week. . . . WNBC's investigative reporter Scott Weinberger discovered, in questioning the 14 men, the federal officers failed to uncover a key piece of information. FBI members and immigration people sat

down with these men. They questioned them. And of course, afterwards, they said, "Everything checked out." But everything didn't really check out. These people [federal agents] missed something as simple as visas that were expired. How did that happen?

WEINBERGER: . . . My sources are telling me that each individual member they talked to, these 12 people or so, the 14, they took their visas and made copies of them and put them in a file as part of an investigation. But. . . the investigators never looked down to check the date. The expiration was three weeks prior to the flight ever taking off.

SCARBOROUGH: That's remarkable! So you have immigration officials there. You have FBI officials there . . . Law enforcement people swarming around these men. And the most basic of questions, "Are you in the United States legally?" was a question that they botched. I would guess the FBI and [ICE] have to be very embarrassed by what you've uncovered.[25]

Weinberger told Scarborough that his sources informed him that agents from ICE had met the plane. Later, ICE would tell Congress that they ignored protocol and did not meet the plane. Statements ICE would make to other mainstream news outlets picking up on the story simply wouldn't add up. Dean Boyd, spokesman for ICE, the FAMS's parent agency, told NPR's Mary Louise Kelly[26] that on the day of the flight, thirteen of the fourteen men (one was a U.S. citizen[27]) were in fact traveling on expired visas. Later that same day, a different ICE official called NPR back to say the previous information was incorrect—that an extension for the Syrians' visas had been granted by the time they flew.

The contradictory information was no credit to an agency already under attack for a spate of snafus in which terror suspects had strolled freely across U.S. borders.[28] An editorial in the *Washington Times* summed up how unsafe this kind of misinformation about flight 327 made people feel: "The flip-flop by DHS is just the latest odd twist in a story that raises troubling questions about the ability of our immigration authorities and airline security apparatus to keep potentially dangerous people off passenger planes."[29]

The *9/11 Commission Report* had revealed that immigration authorities had failed to prevent 9/11. At Congress' behest,[30] the immigration service had undergone a major restructuring and been given its own law enforcement arm, ICE. And now, nearly three years later, immigration authorities were failing all over again. As Steven Emerson, considered one of America's leading authorities on terrorism, commented to Scarborough on Weinberger's report:

> Look, Joe, the fact of the matter is that this is a major embarrassment. These are Syrian nationals, who are on a country, one of the seven countries, that officially supports terrorism. They were out of status.
>
> And then when they landed at the airport in Los Angeles, nobody interrogated them. They were allowed

to leave as if they were just American citizens or they were foreigners coming from Europe. The reality is, this is a scandal that really needs to be investigated. And I can tell you, having spoken to FBI agents in the field, they are telling me, go get them. Because, Joe, this needs to be exposed. Because headquarters is trying to basically pretend it wasn't a scandal.[31]

Things were going from bad to worse for the federal agencies that were trying to make flight 327 go away. But nothing put the nail in the coffin like Audrey Hudson's July 22, 2004, piece in the *Washington Times*, "Scouting Jetliners for New Attacks; Crews Cite Suspicious Arab Passengers." The article was a watershed. Until then, I had been the lone voice suggesting that dry runs were happening on commercial airplanes. Hudson's article changed all that. The lead line in the article couldn't have been worse news for those intent on denying that this kind of thing was going on: "Flight crews and air marshals say Middle Eastern men are staking out airports, probing security measures and conducting test runs about airplanes for a terrorist attack."

In addition to referencing flight 327 in her article, Hudson backed up her opening salvo with several disturbing accounts from pilots and flight crew members who had witnessed suspicious activity on other flights and reported it to superiors. Among these accounts was one particularly disturbing report from an air marshal: A Middle Eastern passenger had been in an aircraft bathroom far too long, and the air marshal on board became suspicious. He forced his way inside the bathroom and discovered that the passenger had removed the bathroom mirror and was attempting to break through the wall and into the cockpit.[32]

For me, Hudson's story raised the question, *why hadn't this been reported before?* Later, I interviewed Hudson about this. Why, I asked, hadn't she run with the information earlier? She replied: "The morning your story broke, I'd been emailed the article by several pilots. But I didn't read it; it was from the Internet. Then, later in the day, Dave Mackett [president of Allied Pilots' Safety Association] called me and he said, 'Audrey, you've *got* to read this'—he was of course talking about your story. I read it and I was shocked because you laid out every single warning sign I'd learned on my beat. You see, before that, I'd been told a couple of similar things—about these dry runs. But you know there's the old journalists' saying: 'one's a rumor, two's a trend, three's a story.' Well, after I read your piece, suddenly, I realized I had a story."[33]

Meanwhile, the FAMS's management adamantly denied that any such thing was going on. Dave Adams gave this statement to the press: "We have no specific intelligence information that terrorist groups are conducting test flights or surveillance activity."[34]

The agencies involved in handling flight 327 were coming across in the mainstream media like the Keystone Cops. With so much negative press, they switched tactics and set about discrediting me. Only one week earlier, Dave Adams had told Joe Scarborough, "I applaud Annie Jacobsen for notifying the flight attendants about the situation."[35] And then suddenly unnamed government sources were saying the problem on the flight was me.

The FBI and the FAMs hit hard. "It's significant [that] the alarm on the flight came from a passenger," FBI spokesman Cathy Viray told reporters. "The complaint did not stem from the flight crew."[36] A FAMS source, someone purportedly "close to the secretive federal protective service," told the press that "the passenger, later identified as Annie Jacobsen, was in danger of panicking other passengers and creating a larger problem on the plane."[37]

Even more outrageous, the "source" claimed that "the air marshals on the flight were partially concerned Jacobsen's actions could have been an effort by terrorists or attackers to create a disturbance on the plane to force the agents to identify themselves."[38]

The FAMS and the FBI knew this was categorically untrue. They had access to my statement from the airport—the one which I'd signed, raised my right hand, and taken an oath that it contained nothing but the truth. I made it clear that I never once spoke to a flight attendant or crew member during the flight. I sat quietly in my seat, only once getting up to use the rear bathroom. I looked around the plane a lot, yes, but despite what I was feeling about what was happening, I didn't let it show. I remained calm so that I would not alarm my son, as any mother would.

In the next few weeks, I would have at least three conversations with the FBI. Each time, I spoke with the same person, spokesman Cathy Viray. I didn't realize at first that she was the "source" who had made the false statement about me to the press. When I finally figured it out, I called her. She seemed like a reasonable person, I told her. What motivated her to make such a categorically false statement, one that clearly would have a profound effect on my ability to report on the story with credibility? I told Ms. Viray that based on the facts from the classified reports she had access to—the flight attendants' statements, the air marshals' statements, and my own sworn statement—she had to have known that I never said a word.

"I was misquoted," she told me sheepishly. There was a long silence. I didn't need to say anything else.[39]

That the FBI and the FAMS wanted the story to disappear was obvious. They made major errors in their handling of flight 327, and the more attention the story received, the more would be revealed about how they had bungled the operation. But it was out of their hands. The day Hudson's piece ran, I started receiving emails from federal air marshals themselves—emails of support. Those who wrote let me know that I was bringing to light something that had been going on since shortly after 9/11 and was being suppressed. Dry runs, the air marshals told me, were most definitely occuring.

The same day the piece ran in the *Washington Times*, I was scheduled to do a live television interview for CNN's *Newsnight* with Aaron Brown. Earlier that day, Kevin and I taped a segment with the network's line producer—something that would introduce my later, live appearance with Aaron Brown. In talking with the producer, it became clear that he was skeptical of our interpretation of the events on the flight. "What if I told you that federal agents trailed the men to the casino and made sure they played the gig?" he asked cryptically.

The question caught me off guard. It was similar to the question the ABC producer had asked me when the story broke, but it sounded to me like the CNN producer knew something. "If these guys showed up on my doorstep tomorrow and serenaded me," I answered, "I'd still have questions about why they did what they did at 30,000 feet."

I didn't know then what Dave Adams had told CNN earlier in the day in his pre-taped interview for the *Newsnight* segment: "The [FAM] supervisor then went out to the casino, verified again that they were booked there, made sure they were playing at the casino." I wouldn't hear Adams's claim until the next morning when I read the *Newsnight* transcript.

It struck me as odd that Adams delivered this critical information over a week after my first article and at exactly the time the federal agencies had embarked upon their campaign to discredit me. Adams's assertion was repeated on many television shows and in newspaper articles, along with his claim that federal agents trailed the men to their Southern California hotel as well. At the time, I didn't dwell on these claims. The government had its position on what the Syrians were really up to, and I had mine. But many months later, more would come out about this "surveillance" of the men from my flight.

As I was on my way to the studio that evening, I received a phone call from three air marshals. They had emailed me earlier in the day and, based on their email addresses, WWS had verified they were in fact federal agents. Two of the marshals believed flight 327 had been an intelligence-gathering mission, the third said he thought it was the "real deal, only for some reason it had been called off."[40] One of the air marshals had been involved in a similar incident in the air, one that he said made flight 327 look like "CandyLand."

The air marshals explained that, within the FAMS, these incidents were called "probes." They knew I was about to go on CNN and suggested I use the word *probe* on national television. That way, they explained, the federal brass would know that I was talking to people inside the service who knew key facts—people aware of other probing incidents that would categorically disprove the party line.[41]

So I did. In talking about flight 327, I told Aaron Brown, "You know, this is not an isolated incident. They can either be called dry runs or they can be called probes."[42] It was my way of letting the FAMS know that I wouldn't be backing down any time soon.

On July 27, I received a call from The House Judiciary Committee saying the matter had escalated to Congress.[43] To borrow Michelle Malkin's phrase, flight 327 had landed on Capitol Hill.[44]

CONGRESSIONAL INQUIRY

The FAMs's willingness to misrepresent key facts about flight 327 did not begin or end with the mainstream media. The FAMs's upper management took it all the way to a United States senator's office and into both houses of Congress as well. But the scandal that was unfolding involved other agencies. The Department of Homeland Security (DHS) and Immigration and Customs Enforcement (ICE) had been keeping relatively quiet in the press, but now they were under congressional scrutiny as well. The House Judiciary Committee (HJC) had opened an investigation into flight 327.

On Tuesday, July 27, 2004, I got a call from Congress. A few hours after that, I was on speakerphone before the HJC. After introductions were made, the individual leading the investigation told me the committee members were, by now, quite familiar with my article. It was explained to me that the committee has oversight over all federal law enforcement agencies. In other words, anyone who wears a badge answers to them. The committee explained why they were calling me. "We're supposed to be getting our information from the agencies, not from you," they said.

The first thing the HJC asked me to do was to go over all the details of flight 327, which I did. Then the committee asked me to go over all the details of what happened once the flight landed and how various agencies had, in my opinion, handled the situation, which I did. The HJC was also interested to hear that I was now receiving information from pilots, flight attendants, and air marshals, indicating that probes had been happening on commercial aircraft all along. The committee asked if I would share this information with them, which I said I would. In the few weeks since my first article had been published, the webzine had become a clearinghouse for information on probes.

Pamela Little, the webzine's editor in chief, and I set about putting all of the pertinent documents together—testimony from pilots, flight attendants, airline employees, and other passengers—about possible probes. We blacked out information that would identify people who wished to remain anonymous and provided telephone numbers for those who were willing to go on the record. The stack of documents we sent to the HJC was several inches thick.

The same day I testified to the HJC, July 27, the federal agencies involved in flight 327, and now being investigated by Congress, sent out a memo announcing that *they* were briefing any interested congressional staffers regarding, "Potentially Suspicious Activities of Passengers on Recent Flights." One veteran journalist explained the purpose of the memo to me: "The agencies involved want to try and diffuse the fact that they're being investigated." In fact, the memo about the briefing had been "leaked" to this reporter,[45] who in turn passed it on to me. It read: "Tomorrow, July 28, 2004, the Department of Homeland Security (DHS) and the Federal Bureau of Investigation (FBI) will brief interested staff on the Government's response to recently publicized incidents of suspicious activity aboard commercial aircraft.

The briefing will focus on an incident involving members of a musical group from Syria which has received substantial media attention."[46]

The memo stated that "briefers" would include top brass from various departments: Randy Beardsworth, director of operations for border and transportation security from the DHS, Director Thomas Quinn from the FAMS, and the deputy assistant director of the counterterrorism division of the FBI, Willie Hulon.

The HJC had scheduled a private briefing for July 28, to be given—for committee members only—by the agencies involved in flight 327. But when the committee arrived at the hearing room, they were shocked to find it was filled with staffers. My source at the HJC explained the shock, "if you open [the briefing] up to more people, you can't get your specific questions answered. We were all under the impression it was going to be just [the committee] and [the agencies] and our questions. It was not. They had opened it up to staffers, not us." I was also told that, during the briefing, the FBI and the other officials representing the government agencies involved tried to undercut my version of events.[47]

In my very first conversation with Dave Adams of the FAMS, he had brought up what he called an extremely "sensitive" issue, one that was "a matter of national security." Adams told me that "where air marshals sit during a flight cannot be talked about to the press." It seemed like a reasonable request, but I told Adams that I had a lot of questions about exactly that.

I explained to Adams that, during the flight, the flight attendant had told my husband, "air marshals are sitting all around you." (This turned out to be false.) Kevin and I had pieced together that two air marshals were definitely sitting in first class. Were all this true, there was an extraordinary number of air marshals on flight 327. I told Adams that if there really were four or five air marshals on board, perhaps that meant someone *knew* the fourteen Syrians were a potential threat. Adams wouldn't confirm or deny this, only repeating that exactly how many air marshals were on the flight, and where they sat, was SSI (Security Sensitive Information). I was not to discuss it with anyone.[48]

Now it was a month later, and much had transpired. When I spoke to Congress, the issue of the number of air marshals on flight 327 was one of the first things I brought up. The committee assured me that there were only two air marshals on board. I told the committee how cagey Adams had been with me about all this; I would soon learn why.

On August 4, 2004, *Time* published an article about flight 327, "Air Marshals Dispute Key Assertions in Flight 327 account."[49] In the article, one of the air marshals from flight 327 challenged key facts from my version of events. He told *Time* that he and his partner didn't see what I saw, suggesting, in essence, that I had made things up. But the marshals couldn't possibly have seen what I saw because they were seated in seats 2B and 4C—in first class. A galley, a lavatory, two closets, and a bulkhead separated the air marshals from the suspicious movements I had reported—in coach. The marshal's assertion that he didn't see the majority of the things I had reported was *literal*. He and his partner were staring at the cockpit door.

Suddenly, I realized why I had been forbidden to discuss where the marshals were seated on the plane—so I couldn't defend myself. The *Time* interview was a cheap shot. Air marshals are strictly forbidden from talking to the press, so the *Time* interview had to have come at the behest of the the director of the FAMS himself, Thomas Quinn. Quinn had taken advantage of my good faith arrangement with the FAMS. And it didn't end there.

Arlen Specter, Pennsylvania's senior U.S. senator and chairman of the Senate Judiciary Committee, had been following the reporting of events on flight 327.[50] And, as U.S. senators can do, he requested that the FAMS brief him on the flight. One of my contacts slipped me an email, written by a senior staff assistant to Senator Specter, about what the FAMS claimed at that briefing.

The first important item was that the FAMS didn't send Dave Adams to the senator's office. Instead, they sent their number two man, John Novak, second only to Director Quinn. What Novak told a U.S. senator was contemptible: he said that the air marshals on flight 327 were seated "throughout the plane and in first class." And he pushed the same fiction—that "Annie Jacobsen initiated the suspicions." He stated that the FAMS had interviewed the Syrians "all individually," when of course they had not. But Novak did confirm one major error: that it is protocol for ICE to show up, but ICE had not. Novak attempted to deflect criticism from the FAMS by ratting out his superiors at ICE.

Outraged, I sent a letter to Novak and copied a number of others, including Tom Ridge and Senator Specter. I described my indignation at Novak's account of the events on flight 327. I also restated my position that flight 327 had a very real threat on board: flight attendants were scared, passengers were scared, and fourteen Middle Eastern men had compromised security (by congregating in groups) and disobeyed the captain's orders (by standing during descent).

I referenced the many letters I had received from airline personnel and air marshals describing their frustrations in dealing with the FAMS. I ended my letter by asking Novak to re-issue a statement to Senator Specter's office that stated the truth about to what went on flight 327.

I never heard back from Novak. But I did have a conversation with the House Judiciary Committee about the situation. They told me that the FAMS had tried the same snow job on the HJC. The HJC had requested that the FAMS bring the air marshals from flight 327 to the briefing (to answer questions), but the FAMS had not. "We saw right through that," I was told.

Then came the ABC interview. One of the air marshals who was *not* brought in to answer questions from Congress *was* flown across the country, along with the FAMS's head of public affairs, Dave Adams, to tape an "exclusive" interview about flight 327 with *ABC News*. This was the same air marshal who had spoken to *Time*.

I was told the network was going to side with the air marshal, but they would give me a chance to voice my side of the story. I was also informed that ABC's line of questioning would be tough.

Before the interview, I called Dave Adams. He was at the airport, about to catch his flight to Los Angeles for the ABC interview, when I caught him on his cell phone.

"Hi Dave," I said. I told him that for the ABC interview, I was going to announce—on national television—that air marshals sit only in first class.

Adams told me that I could not do that.

I told him I could. And that I would.

Adams tried the *national security* tactic again.

Everyone has a breaking point, and I was nearing mine. I told Adams he was full of sh—. If where air marshals sat was such a matter of national security that it required a gag order on me, then Tom Ridge himself would have to call and tell me so.

Adams tried a different tactic. He asked how I *knew* the marshals were in first class on flight 327?

I explained to Adams that he had underestimated what he had told Joe Scarborough were my "untrained civilian eyes."[51] I told him I knew exactly where the *white* air marshal was sitting—on the left side of the plane two feet from the cockpit door—and approximately where the *black* air marshal was sitting—a few feet back, on the right side of the plane. I told Adams that I also knew exactly how much belly hung over the belt on the white air marshal (the one wearing a pin-striped shirt, I added, for more detail), because I had watched him come into coach and assess the situation for one or two minutes of the four-and-a-half–hour flight.

Adams tried a few other tactics, but I had already made up my mind.

"Have you ever considered coaching your air marshals on telling the truth?" I asked. "You guys keep saying I over-reacted. What about the reality that your air marshals under-reacted?"

Adams said he would consider it.

During my interview with ABC, the line of questioning was indeed tough; in fact, it was downright hostile. I must have repeated the line, "The air marshals couldn't possibly have seen what they claim to have seen because they were sitting in first class staring at the cockpit door," some ten or fifteen times. The show's interviewer was incensed. But one of ABC's line producers—sitting across from me and out of view of the camera—kept giving me the thumbs-up.

The ABC interview never ran. Several months later, when I was researching an article on the FAMS, I discovered that information about where air marshals sit was available on the Internet: I found it through a Google search. It had been open source information all along.

A few weeks after the ABC interview, I received some odd information from one of my air marshal sources. On September 2, 2004, he had received a memo from the squad supervisor in his FAMS field office. The subject line read "NW 327." The memo went like this: "There has been some media coverage of the Syrian Band members that traveled from DTW to LAX a few weeks ago. The FAMS has done an investigation of what occurred on this flight and the report is attached. The report includes statements from the FAMs on board regarding the actions of the Syrians. The FAMs account of what occurred differs greatly from that of the reporter on board. It would appear that the reporter was alarmed more by the fact the men were middle eastern [*sic*] than their actions."[52]

It was hard to believe the FAMS was still spending so much time and energy trying to discredit me. According to my source, when an email goes out to rank-and-file air marshals, it goes out nationwide. Therefore, one could assume every FAM in the country had received this information and the attached report. I passed the information along to Congress and made sure they got the FAMS SSI file from one of my air marshal contacts. What really was the point of the propaganda being spread within the FAMS, I wondered? And who had spent so much time, money, and effort creating this long, detailed report that no one else—not even Congress—got to see? My source at the HJC wondered the same thing.

On September 28, after holding closed-door sessions on flight 327 for two months, Congress made their work public for the first time. In a long letter to Thomas Quinn, they asked the director of the FAMS to answer a list of questions about its policies and procedures. The letter begins like this:

"As you [Quinn] know, the Committee on the Judiciary has oversight responsibilities for the Federal Air Marshal Service (FAMS). We are concerned by the media reports, as well as reports from other sources, detailing the alleged security gaps in air travel. As part of our oversight responsibilities, the Committee has the duty to ensure that the efforts of the FAMS are effective. We also owe a duty to the American public to do everything we can to make certain that air travel is as safe as possible."[53]

The letter goes on to pepper Quinn with questions about everything from potentially dangerous dress code policies, to potentially dangerous airport and hotel check-in policies, to extremely dangerous ammunition, to reports of intelligence-gathering probes on commercial airlines. But in a question I particularly enjoyed, Quinn was asked how *Time* magazine had become more important than Congress: "Why did the FAMS believe that it was appropriate to provide *Time* Magazine access to air marshals on board NW flight 327, while failing to bring those individuals to a Congressional briefing about NW flight 327? If the air marshals are important enough to the facts to present to a national audience, why then, are they not important to a Congressional inquiry?"[54]

The morning the letter was sent to Quinn, I was at the grocery store when the HJC called me. They had just faxed the letter over to Quinn and were now ready to fax it to me. The committee was giving me the opportunity of reading it before other members of the press. I hurried home, read it over, and immediately called Director Quinn's office. I identified myself and asked for a statement about the letter from Director Quinn.

"What letter?" Quinn's secretary asked me.

"The letter from Congress," I explained.

"We haven't gotten any letter from Congress," the secretary told me.

I suggested that she check the fax machine. She did. When she came back to the phone, she sounded flustered.

"We'll have to call you back," she said. Director Quinn never returned my call.

I imagine the kind of behavior the FAMS displayed quashes many a story. But it didn't succeed in putting the lid on this one, because—finally—other passengers from the flight started coming forward with what they had seen. When it was no longer my word against the FAMS's, things started to get really interesting.

3

Reporting Suspicious Behavior

TEN DAYS after the story of flight 327 broke, my husband and I were still the only two witnesses who had come forward. And by day ten, the movement by the FAMS and the FBI to paint me as a hysteric with a wild imagination was well underway. Perhaps the agencies felt enough time had passed since the story went public, and that it had received enough publicity, that if other passengers were going to come forward, they would have. That's not what happened.

HEATHER[1]

On July 23, 2004, the morning after I appeared on CNN, I received an email from Heather, a corporate businesswoman from Detroit. Heather was also on flight 327, seated in first class. In the email, she told me that immediately after the flight landed, her instincts told her to speak to the authorities. Instead, she called her husband from the terminal and told him about the horrifying flight. Three weeks later, Heather's husband heard me discussing the flight on the radio, which is how she was able to get in touch with me.

Heather told me she noticed the men behaving suspiciously in the airport waiting area: "Some of the men appeared to know each other, while others acted as if they didn't know each other." Later in the waiting area, she watched as some of the men exchanged glances. "They would look around and catch the eye of someone," Heather said. Other men kept moving around the boarding area, "sitting down and then getting up and changing seats."

Heather boarded the plane and took her seat in first class, feeling uneasy. "I saw enough to make me extremely nervous," she said. During the meal service, Heather watched the man in the green track suit with Arabic writing on the back "come rushing up to first class." There was already one Middle Eastern man in the bathroom and a second man, apparently not with the group, was waiting in line. "But the man in the track suit, literally pushed his way to the first class bathroom, almost knocking [over] the guy who had been waiting," Heather told me. She also felt the man in the green tracksuit stayed inside the bathroom "much too long"—as long as it took her to eat her entire meal. After the Middle Eastern man came out of the bathroom, another man got right up and went inside. Heather told me she thought this man was an air marshal.

According to Heather, the Middle Eastern men "kept coming up front to use the bathroom." The constant foot traffic and strange behavior she witnessed in the front cabin frightened her. Heather spoke on the record about the flight to NPR and the *Washington Times*. "I thought I was going to die," she told the *Times*.[2]

CARL[3]

That same morning, I received an email from Susan.[4] Susan told me that her husband, Carl, and their fourteen-year-old daughter were on flight 327. Her husband is not a small man, she said. In fact, he is quite tall and very strong and "isn't someone who gets afraid." But when Susan picked them up from the airport, Carl was shaken. He told Susan the story of what had happened on the flight, and he said that he was "scared to death." Carl told Susan that if the men had stormed the cockpit all at once, "there would be almost nothing any one on the plane could do because there were so many of them."

I called Susan, and she put me in touch with her husband, forty-eight years old and a resident of Southern California. Carl had been traveling home from Detroit with the couple's daughter. Carl told me that he noticed the men in the boarding area. What he saw made him uncomfortable. "Early on I didn't like what I saw," Carl explained. "It was strange that at first they acted like they didn't know each other, and then they acted like they did." Carl told me he thought the group included about eight men. He was very surprised to learn there were fourteen of them.

Carl was sitting in 26B, over the plane's wing and two rows back from the emergency exit. Ten of the Syrians were sitting within six rows of him. Before the plane took off, the flight attendant stood right near Carl and made an announcement to the people sitting in the row next to the emergency exit door. Carl explained: "She announces how you have to be fit and able, and it's obvious the [Middle Eastern] guy sitting by the exit door doesn't speak English, he doesn't understand what she's saying, so she says, 'Sir you'll have to change seats.' Across the aisle, one of the other Middle Eastern guys jumps up and says, 'I'll switch seats with him.' And he did."

Carl noticed how many trips the men took to the bathroom. He also noticed how they congregated in the aisles. But it was the plane's approach to Los Angeles that stood out for Carl: "What bothered me the most was when we were coming in [to LAX], that last half-hour. My daughter was very upset. My daughter kept asking me, 'Why aren't they sitting down?' I was just trying to keep her calm. I was wondering, 'what is going on? The seat belt light is on, get in your seats.' That's when I thought there was really something going on. I figured at that point, even if they weren't armed, there were enough of them standing that they could break through the cockpit door."

Carl wasn't interested in talking to anyone else from the media. But he did speak to the Department of Homeland

Security when they finally contacted him in March 2005. One year later, Susan and Carl's daughter still refuses to fly.

MARK[5]

As I was waiting to tape *Scarborough Country* on August 2, 2004, I received a call from Mark, a high school football coach, also from California. Mark forwarded me his itinerary; he was seated in coach, in seat 35c—right next to three of the Syrian men. Seated in the back of coach, Mark saw some things I didn't see. I asked him if he thought the men's behavior was suspicious. "Suspicious?!" Mark said, "Absolutely I thought it was suspicious. I've never seen a flight with so much suspicious activity." I asked Mark if he could be a little more specific: "A couple of these guys stood up talking to their buddies almost the whole flight. The flight attendant kept telling them to sit down. At one point right before landing—they had already made the announcement, we'd been cleared for landing—she yelled, 'Sir, you need to sit down, now!' She actually was yelling at him."

I asked Mark how close the plane was to Los Angeles Airport when this happened—when the men were standing on approach. "Close? We were almost there!" Mark explained to me. "I'm a football coach, I'm visiting with these two teenagers nearby—that's how I am—I'm saying, 'look there's a golf course there, there's a high school there, there's a football field there,' and the flight attendant keeps yelling at this guy to sit down."

Once the plane landed, it took Mark a while to get off the plane. First, he thanked the captain, as he always does, and then he walked down the jetway to the door of the gate. That's when he spotted "about a dozen LAPD officers." Interested in what was happening, Mark walked over to where he could see better. "There are these guys getting out their ID's and handing them over to the police. I see these guys, and they're not very concerned. It's not normal, if you're innocent, aren't you going to be upset that you're being taken in?" Mark headed to the baggage claim to retrieve his golf clubs. He waited in the oversize baggage area until the very end. "I never saw any of the Syrians come get any bags," he told me.

Mark flies a lot and he's never seen anything like flight 327. "When I got off the plane," he explained, "the first thing I did was call my wife and my parents. I said, turn on the TV, this is going to be big news."

Mark appeared on *Scarborough Country* and discussed what he saw on flight 327. In March 2005, he spoke to the Department of Homeland Security: they visited him at his home north of Los Angeles. Mark told DHS that he waited a long time at the baggage claim until his golf clubs came. He also told DHS that he didn't see a single musical instrument case come down the oversize baggage chute.

CHARLES AND KATE[6]

Charles and Kate were traveling from Detroit to Santa Monica on a business trip. Normally, the couple flies in first class, but flight 327 was full on June 29, and so they were seated in coach, near the front of the cabin. Charles has spent his long business career traveling on planes to Europe. But this time, right after boarding, he immediately had an "eerie feeling of something not quite right." Kate explained it like this: "Even though we don't believe in any racial profiling, we had to be blind not to notice the interesting seating arrangement of the passengers and the corresponding ethnicities. They were seated in an almost 'z' format." Kate noticed the men were "constantly checking watches, getting up and crossing the aisles to speak in hushed tones." Charles spent "a good part of this very long flight standing in the galley." Kate thinks other passengers "may have mistaken him for an air marshal."

After I received their email, I tried repeatedly to contact this couple, but they didn't write further. I am certain this couple is who they say they are, because I definitely remember a man standing in the galley, watching the Syrians for a good part of the flight. His arms were crossed in front of him, and he looked like he meant business. Other passengers noticed Charles, too.

BILLIE JO[7]

Billie Jo is a certified public accountant who lives in Oxnard, California. She introduced herself to me by remarking, "I'm one of the most boring people I know. This was not my imagination." Billie Jo was so terrified by what happened on flight 327 that she sent two emails to the Department of

Homeland Security telling them about the flight. She never heard back. After she told her father about the flight, he told her about having heard me on a talk radio show.

Billie Jo was in seat 21C. Three of the Middle Eastern men were sitting near her. The man in the track suit with Arabic writing was in the aisle seat directly behind her (22C), another man from the group sat right next to her (21B) and another man from the group, the man with the goatee, sat one row in front of her.

"Immediately, when we were up in the air, they started walking up and down the aisles," Billie Jo told me, "and making this eye contact. The thing that really got me was the eye contact. It was so subtle. If you know somebody, you look at them. You nod your head. That's not what these guys were doing. They were doing these little looks and head signals—acknowledging each other, and yet pretending not to know each other."

Another detail Billie Jo found odd was that the man next to her seemed to be pretending to be asleep. I asked Billie Jo what she meant by this, and she explained that when "one of his buddies would walk by," the sleeping man would open his eyes just a little and look up. "They were all doing this little eye thing, and this little head thing," Billie Jo explained. "A couple of the other guys were going up and down the aisles looking at each other, making those head signals. They were signaling to each other, that was *really* freaky."

Billie Jo noticed the McDonald's bag: "It was so big, and I thought, how many burgers does he have in there?" Billie

Jo also watched the man with the limp. "It was more than a limp," she told me, "it was a dragging of the foot."

But the most alarming detail of all—a detail which Billie Jo emailed to DHS: "The tall man in the jogging suit sat right behind me," Billie Jo explained. "He got up and passed by me to go to the bathroom up in first class. The man was gone for a very long time. And when he came back, he reeked of chemicals—the chemicals from the toilet bowl. He absolutely reeked of it." I asked Billie Jo if she was sure about this. "It's not something you forget," she explained. "I thought, what was he doing in the toilet? He didn't smell like chemicals when he got up to go to the bathroom—it was when he came back. It was so spooky. What was he doing in there that he would smell so strong of chemicals from the toilet?"

By the time the flight was about to land, Billie Jo was terrified. "I thought, 'this is it,'" she told me. "I hear this flight attendant say, 'Sir, stay in you seat.' She was strapped into her seat—it was on the microphone. She said again, 'Sir, stay in your seat,' and again, 'Sir, stay in your seat!'"

I asked Billie Jo how many of the men were standing during the final approach. "I was afraid to look around," she said. "Quite frankly, I thought to myself, 'Well, this is it.' At this point, I was doing some praying. I know it sounds chicken, but that's what I was doing."

When the flight pulled up to the gate, Billie Jo wondered why the plane went to the first gate: "Since I didn't think Northwest had a hub in Los Angeles, I didn't think we'd get the first gate. Now I think I understand. I think they took us to the first gate to make it easier for the officials to get to the plane, but I don't know for sure. When I first got off the plane, I said, 'Thank you, God.'"

Billie Jo went to the FBI website and tried to file a report with them. "The FBI's site requires you to submit your name and contact information, and I got cold feet. But then I went to the Department of Homeland Security's website, and like I said, I emailed them the information about the man smelling like chemicals."

Billie Jo wasn't happy to learn that no one bothered to check the Syrians visas at LAX. "Not after 9/11," she told me. "Before 9/11, we lived in an almost Shangri-La. After 9/11, it should be different. Why am I taking my shoes off if they're not checking visas?"

She also wondered why the government hadn't interviewed everyone from the flight. If they did, she reasoned, they would know there really was a threat on board. She had exchanged many glances with other passengers: "Many other people noticed something was happening."

KEVIN JACOBSEN[8]

Each passenger who contacted me noticed different details, all interesting, all troubling. My husband, Kevin, had his own experience. Kevin noticed the group of Middle Eastern men in the boarding area right away. "Two had instruments and the other had a large McDonald's bag. I thought, why wouldn't you eat your McDonald's before you got on the plane. It's not exactly food that gets better as it gets cold."

Sitting in his seat before take-off, he watched as people boarded. "I watched intently what they did, how they checked in with the guy in the yellow shirt, and my gut said 'Something is not right.' My gut said 'Take your family and get off this plane.' Then the guy with the limp tries to change seats at the last possible moment. It's not right, but I don't have the guts to follow through with my instinct and get my family off the plane. The wheels roll back and I think, 'Now I'm stuck here.' I actually thought, 'Kevin, you didn't have the guts to stand up and simply remove your family from the plane,' and that's when I thought about faking a heart attack so that I would have a good enough excuse to get my family off the plane."

Kevin found the McDonald's bag very strange: "It was forty-five minutes *at least* from the time the guy could have bought the McDonald's to the time he starts eating it, once we're up in the air. I watch him start to eat a hamburger. He wasn't eating it, he was forcing himself to eat it. He held his hand up to his mouth, and he was gagging. Then he puts the burger in the bag and goes into the bathroom, and I think, he's going to throw it out, but instead, he comes out of the bathroom with the bag, slightly smaller now, and he walks to the back of the plane with it, passes his friends, gives the thumbs, up, and then, as soon as he passes this one guy, that guy gets up, goes into the overhead and gets something out. It was orchestrated—at least that's how it looked to me."

Kevin was the only passenger on the plane I interviewed to notice the suspicious man in first class. When DHS visited us nine months later, they asked Kevin a lot of questions about this man. Here's how Kevin describes him: "He looked hipper than everyone else. He wasn't tall, maybe 5'5" with curly-ish hair. Could have been Middle Eastern or not. But he stood so much, and he was so close to the cockpit door, when people came out of the bathroom up there in first class, he had to move. He kept talking to the flight attendants. It was unnatural to talk to them this much, unless he knew them. It was over the top how much he was talking to them." The man kept his sunglasses on for the entire flight.

Later in the flight, the men were walking up and down the aisle. "It was like they were patrolling," Kevin explained. "There were two guys in the back, a guy standing in the front, and some guys walking the aisles, noting how many people there were, like they were counting passengers. I took my pen out and I held it in my hand. I held my pen in my hand for the rest of the flight."

Kevin shared these details with the FBI and the FAM supervisor at the airport. He told the FAM supervisor about wanting to get off the plane before take-off, that his instinct told him to remove himself from the plane, but he didn't have the courage to say so, and that he considered faking a heart attack even as the wheels rolled back. To this, the FAM supervisor said, "Trust your gut. If you ever feel like you or your family are in danger, trust it. It doesn't matter if you're on a mountain top or in a shopping mall, remove your family." Then he told Kevin to be sure to drink lots of water and take two aspirin before he went to bed: "You've had four hours of adreneline."

All of these details are in Kevin's sworn statement. When the FBI and the FAMS were working so hard to discredit me, I found it fascinating that they never used the details Kevin shared with them—about the heart attack and the pen. Out of context, a person who considers faking a heart attack could be easily portrayed as a little off-kilter. Out of context, a passenger sitting through a flight with a pen in his hand poised like a weapon could reasonably be considered paranoid. Yet the FBI and the FAMS didn't spin the *truth* about Kevin's actions. Instead, they spun *fiction* about what I had done—or rather, had not done.

AN ONGOING INVESTIGATION

There were now a total of nine passengers on board flight 327 with important details from the flight. Collectively, these details confirmed the general facts: that the Syrians were behaving in a way that indicated there was a real threat on board. Individually, these details illustrated that indeed many strange things had transpired during the flight. That so many passengers were terrified underscores how outrageous it was that the government had simply let the fourteen Syrians go based only on their claim that they were a traveling band of musicians with a gig to get to.

The government didn't take any other passenger statements after the flight landed; that much was clear. But what had they done in the month since, I wondered? I put in a call to Dave Adams and asked him the question that Billie

Jo had asked me: "Exactly how many other passengers on flight 327 have the FAMS or the FBI been in contact with during the past month?"

Adams told me that they had interviewed the air marshals on my flight, as well as all the flight attendants from flight 327—several times.

I told Adams that wasn't my question. I specifically wanted to know how many other passengers the FAMS or the FBI had contacted during the previous month.

Adams claimed that my husband and I were the only two passengers to come forward.

I told him that wasn't true, that I now had information from seven other passengers from the flight.

Adams repeated that no other passengers had been in touch with him. I reminded Adams that, as a federal agent, he had access to the flight manifest. Then I repeated Billie Jo's question: "How many passengers from flight 327 have you contacted?"

Adams said zero.

When I asked him why, Adams said that the air marshals on flight 327 had determined that there was in fact "suspicious activity" on board, but that they determined it wasn't a "threat." Adams told me I was "splitting hairs."

I then asked Adams if the FBI had interviewed any other passengers. He said the FBI considered flight 327 an ongoing investigation.[9]

4

Level One Threats

IN THE MONTHS AFTER FLIGHT 327, flight attendants, pilots, air marshals, and ordinary passengers continued to contact me with their stories of possible terrorist probes on commercial aircraft. Their first-hand accounts all involved unusual and suspicious in-flight behavior by Middle Eastern men. Because airline employees, as well as air marshals, are strictly forbidden to speak to the press, collecting and verifying information is difficult. Nevertheless, there are certain incidents that stand out, not just because of the events themselves, but because of the lack of media coverage and the "official" spin of airline and security personnel.

UNITED 925

One group of individuals agreed to let me tell their stories about a United Airlines flight in June 2004. Most were nervous about talking to me: all United Airlines employees sign strict non-disclosure agreements stating that under no circumstances can they discuss "accidents and incidents" with the press. But the incident they were involved in was so threatening, and the way it was handled so appalling, they felt compelled to speak out.

It was June 13, 2004. Two weeks and two days before Northwest 327. At London's Heathrow Airport, the crew of United Airlines flight 925 was busy helping the last of its passengers settle into their seats. It would be about an eight-hour flight—3,677 miles direct to Washington's Dulles Airport. Flight attendants conducted last-minute safety checks and readied the massive Boeing 777 and its nearly four hundred passengers for take-off. Then, just minutes before the aircraft doors were set to close, ground agents hurried down the jetway with a group of late arrivals.

According to the ground agents,[10] the nine men had arrived independently on separate itineraries from various Middle Eastern countries. The flight crew[11] was told that one man came from Lahore, Pakistan, another from Dubai, United Arab Emirates, and another from Afghanistan. Several of the men had no carry-ons, which one of the flight attendants found unusual. Most passengers embarking on a long, international flight carry at least *something* with them. The flight attendant took the ground agent aside and said, "*something's not right.*"

The ground agent told the flight attendant she was being paranoid. The men, purportedly all Pakistani nationals, had been through secondary screening and had been swabbed for explosives. A heated discussion between the United Airlines ground agent and the flight attendant took place. The flight attendant inquired about what, if any, additional security measures could be taken; the ground agent pressed for an on-time departure. No additional security checks were made, and the flight left on time.

Once the flight was in the air, a flight attendant in the coach class cabin noticed a bag in the aisle. She asked that the owner of the bag identify himself at once. No one came forward to claim the bag. One of the late-arriving Middle Eastern men was seated nearby. The flight attendant asked the man pointedly if the bag was his. He replied "no" in English. Later, this same man approached the flight attendant and said that the bag in the aisle was his and that he wanted it back.

It soon became apparent to the flight crew that at least some of the men knew each other. During the flight, several of the men walked to the mid-section of the plane and stood in a group by the aircraft door. The lead flight attendant notified the captain; the air marshals on board had already been made aware. About the same time, two of the Middle Eastern men, seated in the far rear of the plane, started taking photographs of the aircraft's interior.

The flight attendants now began closely monitoring what the men were doing. One of the men carried a hand-held mirror as he walked around the plane. According to one flight attendant, the man "was holding [the mirror] and moving it around so he could see what was going on behind him. What he was doing was very suspicious."

Another flight attendant noted that the men had electronic gadgets with them. "They were not Game Boys or computers," said the veteran crew member, "but small electronic devices. I didn't recognize what they were." Other flight attendants took notice of the electronic equipment as well—some of which was being passed among the men. "They started passing this one electronic device back and forth," said another flight attendant. "It looked like a transistor radio, only it wasn't."

The crew took turns walking the aisles and monitoring the suspicious activity. "Every time one of the flight attendants walked by, they [the Middle Eastern men] watched us. We were watching what they did and they watched everything we did. I noticed they constantly had their eyes on a crew member," one of the flight attendants noted.

Meanwhile, the captain radioed Heathrow Airport, asking that the men's names be re-checked against the terrorist "no-fly" list. Word came back from the captain to the crew that *two* of the nine men were on the "no-fly" list.

"We were horrified," one flight attendant told me. "I heard the captain wanted to divert—I don't know why we didn't. We made sure the passengers didn't notice, but we were all horrified." According to the crew, the air marshals were keenly aware of the situation. "The air marshals were ready and prepared," said one flight attendant. "Apparently, they had their guns out under their blankets."

The captain requested that the FBI meet the plane in Washington. But when the plane landed, not a single law enforcement officer met the aircraft. No FBI, no ICE, no Joint Terrorism Task Force (JTTF), no airport police. Instead, there was one United Airlines supervisor with a clipboard.

According to the flight crew, the captain was furious. "The pilot went ballistic," said a flight attendant. "The air marshals went ballistic. The captain had requested law enforcement—two of those guys were on the 'no-fly' list—and they [United Airlines] disobeyed captain's orders!"

Without a single law enforcement officer to question the men, all nine suspects—two of whom were possibly a threat to national security—walked off the plane and disappeared into the crowds.

When the flight crew of United Airlines flight 925 landed safely in the nation's capital, they kissed the ground. Then they got angry. One flight attendant explained: "When we landed at Dulles, we expected a whole fleet of people [FBI] to meet the plane. Instead, this regular United [Airlines] supervisor turns up. He stands there with a clipboard and says, 'I'm sorry, guys.' He was pathetic. After what we went through! And the fact that we all had to fly the next day—that didn't matter to him. He says, 'world headquarters says, we're sorry.' *Sorry?* They say safety and security is their priority. Well, it's not."

The crew decided to take action. They got together and compiled a detailed account of the entire series of events— from the pre-flight conversations with ground agents at

Heathrow, to the minute details of the in-flight suspicious activity. "We asked, 'Why wasn't the FBI there? Why couldn't the pilot divert?' We wanted real answers. You know what they told us? They [United Airlines] said, 'Forget about suing. Those guys were FBI plants.' They [United Airlines] put it in an email. It was ridiculous. But what can you do?," the flight attendant said.

Jeff Green, head of media relations for United Airlines, confirmed the broad details of United Airlines flight 925: suspicious behavior by a group of men, congregating near the aircraft door and taking photographs inside an aircraft cabin.[12]

I asked Green how it was possible that not a single law enforcement agent met the plane: "Wouldn't this have been disobeying the captain's orders?" Green's answer? "There are times when law enforcement is requested, but they don't show up." Green also told me that the flight was determined to be a "level one threat" and that law enforcement isn't necessarily required to show up for a "level one threat." I asked what "level one" meant, and Green said, "You'll have to ask DHS."

David Mackett, President of the Airline Pilots' Security Alliance (APSA) and also a captain for a major airline, finds Green's reasoning hard to believe. "If a captain requests law enforcement, law enforcement always shows up, and usually in droves," Mackett said, adding "The captain is completely responsible for the safety of the flight, its passengers and crew."[13]

I asked Green about the captain's statement that two of the men were on the "no-fly" list. Green confirmed that in the captain's written report, the captain stated that two of the men were on the "no-fly" list. But Green also told me that the captain's information did not match up with the information *other* United Airlines employees had. According to Green, the names of the nine men were checked against the airline's "no-fly" list before the plane left London. And then, at the captain's request, the names were re-checked against the "no-fly" list, while the flight was over the Atlantic, but "the information did not match up."

"So where did the captain get his information?" I asked. Green told me he didn't know, but again repeated, "United re-checked the list, and the information did not match up."

Green's words, *the information did not match up,* sounded uncannily familiar to me. The morning of my conversation with Green, the AP wire had quoted him saying essentially the same thing about another United London-to-Washington flight—the one from which Yusuf Islam, formerly known as Cat Stevens, was removed.

Instead of landing in Washington as scheduled, the flight carrying Islam was diverted to Bangor, Maine, where the British national was removed from the plane by FBI agents. The Transportation Security Administration (TSA) announced Islam was on the "no-fly" list. Publicly, both the DHS and the TSA pinned the blame for the security debacle squarely on United Airlines, saying its employees had failed to properly check the "no-fly" list. But Green fiercely defended the airline's position, telling the press that United Airlines employees *did* check Islam's name against the information on *their* list, but "the information did not match up."

I asked Green if the DHS was notified of the incidents on United Airlines flight 925. Green assured me it was. "We did follow through with DHS," Green said. "We followed procedure."

The DHS refers all airline-related questions to the TSA, so I called Mark Hatfield, director of communications for the TSA. I asked Hatfield why law enforcement did not meet United Airlines flight 925, despite the captain's orders, and whether the two men onboard were indeed on the "no-fly" list. He promised to "get on it." The next day, Hatfield sent me an email, saying: "I'm waiting for my ops folks to get back to me. Please stand by." Despite many follow-up calls (eight) and emails (four) from me, no word from Hatfield for nearly three weeks.

I called Hatfield one last time. He took my call and apologized for not getting back to me earlier. He discovered that there was no report on United 925: "We got no reports on that day on that flight. I went to various offices who receive incident reporting—and there's a lot of it—but going back through the tapes and records, on that day for that flight, there's nothing."

"So you're saying United didn't report flight 925 to you?" I asked. Hatfield said no, that there was nowhere else the information could have gone.

I asked Hatfield if the men on the flight really were FBI plants. He said, "I have no knowledge of that. It's not something I've heard about around here." I asked what constituted a "level one threat." He said off the top of his head he didn't know, but he'd look into it.

With no word back from Hatfield on "level one" threats, I again called Jeff Green at United Airlines and left a detailed message. Later in the day Green left me this voice mail message: "Annie, hi. This is Jeff Green with United Airlines. Got a message that you had called and I talked with Mark Hatfield with the U.S. government and did indeed find out that a level one threat is a term that United [Airlines] uses, not necessarily one that TSA uses, to determine different threat levels based on what's going on on the airplane. I see that you are calling to confirm that, and you want to know what a level one threat entails. I'm not going to provide you with that information. That's information that we don't provide publicly because it is secure and sensitive. When we determine certain levels of threat, we're not going to share that outside the company. Unfortunately, I can't give you any more info on the subject. I think we've talked about it enough."[14]

So "level one threat" is a United Airlines term, one that Green doesn't seem to have been familiar with during our first conversation. Someone at *United Airlines*, then, categorized the flight as a "level one threat," having decided that *his* opinion of what was happening on board was more important than the captain's.

BRITISH AIRWAYS 0215

In April 2005, I received an email from Barry Johnson, a blogger from CynicalNation.com, who related a bizarre incident that happened at London's Heathrow Airport. Barry contacted me because he had read "Terror in the Skies Again?"

On April 3, 2005, his brother-in-law was sitting on the tarmac waiting for British Airways flight 0215 to depart for Boston's Logan Airport when heavily armed men came on board and removed two passengers of Middle Eastern descent by force. The rest of the passengers were then removed from the plane and taken to a special area of the airport for several hours. Five hours later, the passengers boarded a different plane. They arrived at Logan Airport without further incident.

The next day, both Barry and his brother-in-law were surprised that they did not see any mention of the incident in the media. Barry posted a brief account on his blog and got a few inquiries. Then he contacted me: "I called British Airways to ask them about the incident, and they told me they couldn't say anything about it . . . still no mention of this in the media. I'm beginning to wonder how often this goes on, and we simply never hear about it."[15]

I called my contact at British Airways. Eventually, I spoke with Vice President of Corporate Communications John Lampl. I identified myself and asked for a statement from BA on the incident. "Oh, that," Lampl said nonchalantly. "That was a case of a nervous passenger not wanting to fly."

I asked Lampl if he could elaborate.

"The passenger was nineteen years old, and apparently he was feeling apprehensive about flying. He was with a relative—his cousin or brother, I think—and the relative conveyed that he wasn't comfortable flying, so he was de-planed."

"The relative deplaned?" I asked.

"No, the nineteen-year-old. He didn't fly."

I explained to Lampl that I had a passenger witness who told me that the men were armed.

"The passengers were armed?" Lampl asked.

"No, the agents who came on board were armed," I explained.

"Oh, yes, they were," said Lampl, again without missing a beat.

"So let me get this straight," I said. "Armed agents—and British cops don't carry weapons—came on board to remove a passenger who *requested* to get off?"

"That's correct," Lampl said.

"That doesn't sound correct," I told Lampl, but that was all he had to say.[16]

Johnson put me in touch with his brother-in-law, pas-senger-witness John.[17] John is the executive vice president of a software company and flies frequently all over the world. He gave me his account of the incident.

"Well, the door was shut; we hadn't yet pulled away. We're all seated, seat belts on, and the captain comes on and says, 'We have a security issue to deal with. While we sort it out, you can all use your cell phones and the bathrooms.' About forty-five minutes later, the captain comes back on and says, 'there are some passengers who are about to board the plane so if you could all take your seats.'

"Naturally, I was expecting some late passengers. Now, I was in the back of the plane so I had a very good view. Actually, I was in the same aisle as what went on. So the door opens and this guy—security—comes running up. Running. And his gun is drawn. It's a machine gun. He's dressed army-style, he has a crew-cut, a bullet-proof vest, and a machine gun out like he's going to shoot someone. Behind him is another guy, a bobby cop, and he's got his pistol out and aimed. Then there's a flight attendant, and after that, there's another SWAT guy dressed the same, in a bullet-proof vest with the machine gun."

I interrupted: "A machine gun? I'm no gun expert, but a machine gun? Can we be sure about this?"

John told me that as a software executive, he too is unfamiliar with weaponry, but he was confident about the machine gun. "Look," he told me, "these guys were straight out of central casting. I mean it was something out of the movies. They had that quasi-military look and the big automatic weapons. Everyone was shocked. People with guns out are not what you expect to see when you're sitting on a plane. They rushed on board. It was quick, smooth, and alarming."

I asked John to continue.

"So, they rush up to the row that I'm in—except the passenger was across the aisle. They point the guns at the passenger in the middle seat, and the guy with the machine gun says, 'You! Come with me!' and then—this part is funny, really—the flight attendant says, 'No! Not him. Him!' and points to another passenger, the guy sitting in the next seat over—by the window."

John told me that before the police rushed the plane, he hadn't even noticed the young man. I asked him to describe the passenger at whom the officers were pointing their guns and how he reacted.

"He was young, maybe nineteen. He was Middle Eastern, darkish skin, dark hair. He didn't put up a fuss of any kind. He looked startled but not totally shocked. He was pretty meek. He didn't make any sudden moves. . . . These guys with the guns were serious. The passenger got his bag out of the overhead cabin and left [the plane]."

"They let him get his bag himself?" I asked. (In the U.S., TSA won't let passengers even touch their bags during pre-boarding searches, let alone when they're being escorted off a plane.)

John replied, "The guy said something like, 'Can I get my bag out of the overhead?' and then he did. He kind of quietly gathered up his things and left. The passengers sitting next to him had been cleared out of the way so it was just this guy and then the agents with their guns on him."

I asked John what happened next.

"I was seated next to the bulkhead, so I could see the bathroom. One of the SWAT team guys stayed behind. He went inside and started searching the bathroom. He opened all the compartments. I saw him stick his hand into the garbage and fish around inside.

"Then the captain came back on. He said, 'As you can see, we had someone removed from the plane. Please remain seated. We're going to get a new plane.' Then he said something about safety being British Airways' first concern. About ten minutes later, he comes back on and says, 'We are getting a new plane,' and that we'll all get a voucher for dinner. Oh, and if we don't want to fly on to Logan just now, British Airways will honor that.

"When we deplaned, there were all kinds of people. Police and British Airways-type people. There were three or four bobby cops. And maybe five to eight official looking people. All along the path to the waiting area, there were people stationed, so it clearly wasn't some tiny thing.

"Four hours later, we re-board. It was the same crew, same captain. The captain comes on and says, 'To tell you a little more, our cabin crew identified two individuals who were acting suspiciously, and we had them removed from the plane.' Then he said something like 'and it was a good thing.'"

I asked John if he ever saw the second individual.

"No, the first I learned that there were two people was when the captain made that announcement. I only saw the one guy. I never saw this other passenger. I was in the coach cabin, and he wasn't anywhere that I could see."

I repeated what the British Airways spokesman had told me, that the passenger had *asked* to be removed.

"The guys who came on board were serious. I felt like they wanted to make sure this person wasn't going to take a hostage. They were aggressive. The way they were acting, it was like they were prepared in case somebody said, 'I have a bomb.'"

The story from British Airways doesn't add up. Why does a passenger who changes his mind about flying—which happens a lot—require an armed escort off the plane? And why did the airline provide a different plane for the flight?

All this comes on the heels of Heathrow's announcement that it has relaxed many of its post-9/11 security measures. They've reintroduced metal knives into first-class dining and will soon be allowing passengers to travel with scissors and blades under three inches long.

I called the DHS about flight 0215 and was told the incident was ICE's jurisdiction. The TSA never returned my call. Britain's equivalent of the DHS, MI-5, never got back to me.

The official nonchalance, spinning, and stonewalling on the part of the airlines and the authorities raises the question: Will we ever know how often these incidents occur? Twice a year? Once a month? Every day? If straight answers aren't forthcoming about an incident to which there were witnesses, is there any hope of shining a light on what's really going on and the progress—or lack thereof—in airline security? Wouldn't British Airways benefit from the publicity—if in fact they removed a potential threat. And if the man really was just another nervous flyer, why a new plane?

No more information about British Airways 0215 was forthcoming, but it was an interesting week for airline security news. On April 8, 2005, there was a terror scare aboard KLM flight 685 as it traveled from Amsterdam to Mexico City. A few hours into the flight, DHS officials discovered two of its passengers are on one of the U.S. government's lists of known terror suspects. The men, Saudis, were brothers. They are also pilots—pilots who attended the same flight school as the 9/11 hijacker Hani Hanjour. In previous discussions with the U.S. government, these two Saudi brothers had admitted to being friends with other members of the 9/11 plot.

U.S. officials refused to let flight 685 enter U.S. airspace. The Mexican government followed suit, and the flight, carrying 293 passengers and a few horses, returned to Amsterdam. The two men told authorities they were traveling to Mexico City to visit their ailing father, a former Saudi diplomat.[18] They were questioned extensively—and released.

5

"The Syrian Wayne Newton"

THE FIRST ARTICLE ABOUT FLIGHT 327 to appear in a major newspaper was written by Joe Sharkey for the *New York Times*. Sharkey began the piece by stating, "There is no doubt something out of the ordinary happened on Northwest Flight 327." He spent the rest of the lengthy article presenting an "either/or" scenario, wondering if the flight was a "prelude to terrorism or passenger paranoia." Sharkey also managed to underscore a bizarre aspect of the story. The "band" that had become the subject of a world-wide media storm had not come forward. "I couldn't locate the band either, by the way," Sharkey wrote parenthetically.[1] On July 25, 2004, a lengthy article about "Terror in the Skies, Again?" that originally ran in the London *Telegraph* was reprinted, *in Arabic*, in the *Arab Times*.[2]

As various Syrian Bands were misidentified as the one from the flight, their members had come forward to say,

"It's not us, we're not *that* band!" In the first days after the story broke, the Syrian band Kulna Sawa was misidentified (by several bloggers) as being the band from flight 327. The band's manager defended them by providing an alibi: Kulna Sawa members were in Syria on June 29, 2004. In fact, the band's website explains that the group was "not involved in the Air Incident on Flight 327."[3] But no word from the men who actually were on flight 327. It was odd then—and over one year later, still is.

Producers from mainstream news outlets were leaving a trail of posts on English-language, Arab, and Muslim websites—all trying desperately to locate the band. There was a rumor that *Good Morning America* wanted to book the band and have them perform live on national television. And still, no band.

That a reporter for the *New York Times* couldn't locate the band sent others to the task. The next day, in an article published on *National Review Online* (NRO), writer Clinton Taylor identified the men on flight 327 as Nour Mehana and his back-up band. Taylor suggested that "if Jacobsen was wondering why one man in a dark suit and sunglasses sat in first class while everyone else flew coach, well, it seems pretty clear that this was the Big Mehana himself."[4] Taylor was partially incorrect: Mehana was not on the flight.[5]

In his article, Taylor wrote, "I talked to James Cullen of Anthem Artists who confirms that Nour Mehana's large band did arrive on Northwest Flight 327." Cullen, the promoter for the gig, also explained that the band was scheduled to play at an Indian gambling casino called Sycuan, which was located just outside San Diego. After the NRO article was published, Cullen refused to give further interviews. He wouldn't talk to the major newspapers that were pursuing him, to the television stations that kept calling his secretary, or to me.[6] Months later, when I did manage to speak with Cullen, he told me DHS agents had instructed him not to talk to the press.

With the men identified, some felt that the mystery of flight 327 was solved. For me, it was only the beginning.

A THOROUGH INVESTIGATION

All along, it had been a refrain of the FAMs that their investigation had been thorough. According to Adams, a squad of agents at LAX had "thoroughly investigated" the fourteen musicians. The men had been "scrubbed." None had arrest records, none showed up on Homeland Security's "no-fly" list or the FBI's Most Wanted Terrorists List. They were a musical band hired to play a gig at a casino. Everything checked out. The men were interviewed individually for "probably almost two hours," and then they were let go.

Adams told me, as he would later tell the mainstream media, that authorities called the band's promoter (Cullen) to verify the band had a gig. Adams told me, as he would later tell the media, that federal agents "went out to the casino to make sure they were playing." Adams also stated that federal agents went to the hotel where the men were staying and verified that they had reservations. And Adams said that federal agents followed the musicians all the way to the Long Beach airport to make sure they flew back to New York on JetBlue.

Adams told me that if the men traveled back and forth across the country using one-way tickets, which they had, that was their prerogative. If they behaved suspiciously, well, it was "regrettable"—but that's all it was. Adams assured me that the federal agencies involved had done everything that could be done.

During my initial conversation with Adams, I told him I was writing a story. He never asked me not to write the story. Maybe he assumed I would no longer pursue the story once I heard his pitch. Or maybe Adams never thought the story would get out. Maybe he genuinely believed that because these men checked out as a band, because they stayed in a hotel, and because they had airline tickets to New York, there was nothing nefarious about them. Or maybe he was lying about the investigation.

For weeks, I believed what Adams told me. I watched his television appearances, read his statements to the newspapers, and listened to the statements he and other government officials made on the radio. They all worked hard to push the idea that the government had conducted a thorough investigation, that the government had done its job. I doubt I ever shared Adams's understanding of *thorough*, but I was beginning to get the sense that the government's story couldn't hold water.

The first hole in the government's story was revealed in Clinton Taylor's NRO article. "Cullen did receive a follow up email from the Department of Homeland Security," Taylor wrote, "asking him to confirm that the band had played their gig at Sycuan." What a strange claim from the promoter who would soon be silenced. If the DHS had their own agents follow the band to the casino, why would they need anyone else to confirm it? Could the government be lying about its own investigation? It would certainly explain why the DHS had told Cullen to stop talking. And it would explain why the HJC was looking into the matter.

I asked some of my air marshal sources to look into the details of the FAMS investigation. I was shocked to discover that the government had been lying about at least two key points. The Syrian men had not been interviewed "separately" at all. In fact, the FAMS and the FBI agents at the airport interviewed just *two* of the fourteen. Furthermore, the "thorough" investigation had not gone on for "probably almost two hours." Instead, the government had interviewed the two Syrian men for ten or so minutes. Within fifteen or twenty minutes of landing, the men were sent on their way.[7]

THE MUSICAL AMBASSADOR

When Audrey Hudson wrote a front-page story for the *Washington Times* entitled, "Scouting Jetliners for New Attacks," Washington learned that dry runs were likely taking place on commercial aircraft. Among the politicians, lawmakers, and diplomats who could now contemplate this disturbing idea was none other than the Syrian ambassador to the United States, Dr. Imad Moustapha.

After reading the piece, Dr. Moustapha wrote a letter to the editor of the *Washington Times*, which was published on July 26, 2004. Using the royal "we," the ambassador declared shock over Hudson's article, stating that it "only reflects paranoia verging on the point of hysterics." Moustapha also wrote, "The woman mentioned most prominently in this article, Annie Jacobsen, is an advocate of ethnic profiling who survived a horrendous ordeal: a flight with 14 harmless Syrian musicians." Dr. Moustapha was not the first person to accuse me of ethnic profiling. But I was intrigued that Syria's top man in Washington knew that the Syrians on flight 327 were harmless and was willing to say so in print. And so I read on. Of the Syrian musicians on flight 327, Moustapha wrote: "The fact that they have performed in the past six months in places such as the Kennedy Center, the Lincoln Center and the Juilliard School did not prevent Mrs. Jacobsen from saying, 'Couldn't 14 terrorists learn to play instruments?'"[8]

This was truly interesting information. My first thought, when I heard that Moustapha had leaped to the defense of the Syrian band was that he had done so, generally, for patriotic reasons. When I read the specific details of his letter, particularly that Nour Mehana's band had played at three of the most prestigious musical centers in the world, I decided it was time to call Dr. Moustapha myself. I wanted to ask him if he had more information about the "harmless" men on my flight. I wanted to interview the musicians myself. Dr. Moustapha—of all people in the United States—was in the position to put me in touch with them. Not only did Moustapha have his diplomatic position, but he is a man with a thirty-year interest in and involvement with Syrian musicians.

Moustapha's interest in Syrian music is far from casual: he has a website specifically dedicated to discussing his "lifelong infatuation with [Syrian] music"[9]— a passion he has had since he was nine years old. On the site, Moustapha provides links to the many articles he's written about Syrian musicians, as well as the book he has authored on the subject. Imad Moustapha is a veritable authority on Syrian musicians. Not only that, as ambassador, he's been personally involved in bringing Syrian musicians to center stage.

Only a few months before flight 327, in an article in the *Forward* (a revered institution in American Jewish life), "Syria Diplomat Seeking Friends Among Public," Moustapha explained that, in an effort to improve his country's image, he had been "arranging performances by Syrian musicians."[10] My research indicated that a quintet called Hewar had played at the Kennedy Center on February 27, 2004. The event was presented in cooperation with the Embassy of Syria and the Middle East Institute. But my research also indicated that Nour Mehana and his band had never played at Lincoln Center, the Kennedy Center, or the Julliard School, not before and certainly not during the summer of 2004. Why would the ambassador lie about this?

I called the Syrian embassy and after some resistance, the ambassador finally took my call. After introductory pleasantries, I asked Dr. Moustapha why his letter suggested that the fourteen Syrians from flight 327 played at Lincoln Center, the Kennedy Center, and the Julliard School, when they had not.

Dr. Moustapha confirmed that Nour Mehana and his band had *not* played any of these places, but he said that other Syrian musicians had. I told Dr. Moustapha that his letter to the *Times* was at best misleading; Dr. Moustapha told me that I was a paranoid racist.

I asked Dr. Moustapha if, by suggesting that all Syrian musicians are innocent (not to mention talented) just because they are Syrian, he was making the same kind of gross generalization he had accused me of?

Dr. Moustapha told me again that I was a paranoid person and that the men did nothing wrong.

I reminded him that it was the behavior of the men which caused alarm (by then my account had been corroborated by other passengers), not their Syrian heritage.

He said a few more things that aren't fit to print.

I suggested to Dr. Moustapha that we focus on a diplomatic solution. I asked him to please locate the fourteen Syrian musicians in question so that they could share their side of the story. I waited for an answer, but Dr. Moustapha hung up on me.[11]

Eleven months later, Ambassador Moustapha would make headlines again—headlines that seemed rather undiplomatic. In late May 2005, Syria cut all military and intelligence ties with the United States. "We are not cooperating with the United States," Moustapha told CNN's Wolf Blitzer.[12] And then, just a week later, Syrian missile debris hit Turkey—debris from missiles that Israeli military officials told the *New York Times* are designed to deliver chemical weapons in mid-air.[13]

Damascus had no comment for BBC *World News*, and Imad Moustapha had no comment for me when I called him the day after the missiles fell. His secretary informed me that Moustapha wasn't taking calls from the press. Moustapha seemed to have had a change of heart. He had recently told the *Washington Diplomat*, "There's probably no other ambassador as busy as I am," adding, "I spend seven days a week giving media interviews. . . . I have an extremely busy schedule and have only one message: Syria is not an enemy. Stop this negative campaign against Syria."[14]

The negative campaign Moustapha was referring to included ongoing public speculation that Syrians might have been involved in the assassination of former Lebanese prime minister Rafiq Hariri (an outspoken critic of Syria's then-military presence in his country). But instead of addressing the tragic issue with facts or logic, Moustapha had again chosen a finger-pointing, persecution-complex defense.

According to the *Washington Diplomat*, Moustapha has been thrust into the spotlight since Harari's death and has appeared on more radio and television shows than he can remember. When asked who he thought was behind Hariri's murder, Moustapha responded: "I'm not a conspiracy theorist. Nobody knows. However, we can easily see who is benefiting from this crime. The United States is trying to use it to score political points against Syria and allows the criminals who committed this crime to reap the benefits. This is why we are feeling so devastated."[15]

I had been trying all along to get the ambassador to put me in touch with Nour Mehana's band. In one of my follow-up articles for WomensWallStreet.com, I suggested that readers write to the ambassador and encourage him to help me locate the band. I know that hundreds of people did write to him: they copied me on their emails. But the ambassador has never responded to my request.

NOUR MEHANA'S BAND

Nour Mehana, the son of a respected Alawi sheik, used to be a professional reciter of the Qur'an before he became a popular singer. Once he switched careers, his "exceptional voice" rapidly earned him "fame and reverence throughout Syria and the Arab world."[16] His most famous album is *Wala Kan Albal,* which became an instant hit all over the Middle East. One of his most popular songs is called "Um El Shaheed," which in English is "Mother of a Martyr."

Heather Wilhelm, a master's student at University of Chicago, was writing her thesis on Islamic fatwas and martyrdom doctrines right at the time I began to write about flight 327. Intrigued by the story, Wilhelm had the lyrics to "Um El Shaheed" translated by the Middle East Research Institute.[17] The song glorifies the death of a young Palestinian. In the song, Wilhelm explains, "Mehana sings to a grieving mother that she should not be sad because her son, who died a martyr, is a hero. She should be happy that her son is gone ... because freeing Palestine and the Golan Heights are heroic goals." The song ends with a triumphant chorus of Allahu Akhbar, Allahu Akhbar! Wilhelm is correct in pointing out that the questionable lyrics do not mean that Mehana is necessarily involved with dry runs or with terrorism, but they do indicate that he "supports Palestinian intifada—and, along with it, martyrdom doctrines."

After Taylor's article identified the band and their reason for traveling to Southern California, learning about them was much easier. James Cullen wouldn't talk, but I located two more of Nour Mehana's promoters who would. It seems that Mehana and his men had been playing a number of concerts that they had neglected to tell Dave Adams about—or at least that he had neglected to tell me about. In any event, the men flew back and forth across the country quite a bit in the summer of 2004—interesting, considering that their visas had an expiration date of June 10:

- June 18, 2004, Foster City, California: "AMOORA Entertainment and the Bay Area Lebanese Club Presents Nour El Tarab—Nour Mehanna, live in Concert."[18]

- June 19, 2004, Pasadena, California: "Fairouzah-American Association—Nour Mhanna Party."[19]

- July 1, 2004, El Cajon, California: "Sycuan Casino presents Nour Mehana in Concert."[20]

- July 2, 2004, Garden Grove, California: "Transtour Express Proudly Presents Singer Nour Mehana at the Embassy Suites."[21]

- July 4, 2004, North Bergen, New Jersey: the Nile restaurant hosts Nour Mehanna.[22]

I learned from Reza,[23] a promoter involved in several of these concerts, that to book Nour Mehana for an event costs $32,000. Armed with that information, I decided to take a trip down to San Diego to check things out at the casino. If Mehana gave discounts to fraternal organizations like the Bay Area Lebanese Club or the Fairouzah-American Association (a non-profit made up of "generous Syrians" who help those suffering "in the homeland"[24]) it was unlikely he would do so for a casino. It made sense that, if anything, the casino was subsidizing Mehana's trip. I wanted to see what kind of venue could afford a $32,000 event.

At the casino, I set about interviewing the theater manager. I had called ahead and made a non-specific appointment on the way down, but as soon as I started asking questions about Mehana and his band, my visit was cut short by two large security personnel, men who asked me to leave the premises immediately.[25] Instead, I roamed around the casino, searching for an employee who might have seen the show.

Sure enough, I found a woman, Sharin,[26] who had seen the band perform.

Sharin told me a little about the concert. Nour Mehana and his band played for a crowd of about four hundred people. (Another employee at the casino said it was a small crowd, about two hundred people.) Sharin said Mehana sang for two hours and his back-up band played for about half of it. Tickets to the show cost $24 to $30 each,[27] although Sharin paid a little less because she was an employee. That was the extent of the information I got out of Sharin, because that visit was also interrupted by two security personnel, different ones. This time, the men escorted me to the parking lot and made sure I drove away.

On the ride home, I did the math. At an average $27 per ticket for 350 people, the take at the door for the Sycuan show was about $9,450. That puts someone in the hole for $22,550, plus possibly travel, room, and board for fifteen musicians, a tour manager, and at least one promoter. Even if you assume the casino made some money on gambling, food, and alcohol, that's a big negative outlay for a night of Syrian music. I couldn't figure out the cost-effectiveness of flying fifteen men in from Syria for a money-losing event.

Which brought me to another piece of the puzzle that didn't quite fit. In Clinton Taylor's NRO article, Cullen (the promoter) explained that "some of the men came in from Detroit and some from Lebanon." This was odd. Nour Mehana is clearly a marquis singer, known throughout the Arab world (a "Syrian Wayne Newton," as Taylor called him). But for cost reasons, it would make sense that he might use local musicians to back him up, unless, of course, the instruments his musicians played were so rare that no local talent could be found.[28] So who played back-up for Mehana at the June 18 event? Why bring in "some men" all the way from Lebanon, as Cullen stated, when, it was already established, there were folks in northern California who were well-equipped for the job? They weren't exactly playing at the Hollywood Bowl.

Yasmine Yatik[29] is a colorful figure at the Bay Area Lebanese Club. She has coordinated many of the events there, including the Nour Mehana event on Father's Day, June 18, 2004. Yasmine, a Lebanese-American who studied political science in college, spent several hours on the telephone with me, debating the nature of what she called "my accusation" about innocent men on flight 327.

Yasmine was very familiar with Nour Mehana and his back-up band: she hosted the men when they were in town. I asked her if it was true that some of the men came from Lebanon on June 29 and she said yes, some of the men reside in Lebanon, but they carry Syrian passports. I asked her why some of the men would have come straight from Lebanon for the casino gig on July 1, thereby missing her event. And what about the men from her event? Who were they and why weren't they playing at the casino gig? Yasmine insisted that she didn't know anything about the event down south. She didn't have anything to do with it, but as far as she knew, they were "definitely the same band." She told me that the musicians shared their schedule with her. After the Northern California gig on June 18, they were flying to Detroit for "some parties" and then they would be flying back again to

Los Angeles to perform in Southern California.[30] In fact, Yasmine explained, one of the men talked about visiting her again when he was back in California, but never did.

I was beginning to get the sense that Mehana did not always have the same men backing him up—at least not all of them. Indeed, the *New York Times* writer Joe Sharkey had mentioned Nour Mehana as being a popular singer who had "a shifting group of musicians" back him up.[31] So I asked Yasmine about the musician from flight 327 who wore an orthopedic shoe and walked with a very noticeable limp. Yasmine was confused. "No one had a limp," she told me.

I explained that one of the men on flight 327 had an orthopedic shoe and a limp so pronounced it was literally impossible not to notice it. Yasmine said she didn't remember a man with a limp or an orthopedic shoe, but added, "I wouldn't notice something like that anyway."

During a second phone conversation with Yasmine, I again asked her about the man with the limp. She gave me the same answer. Why is this so important, she asked? I explained: according to the TSA website, during the airport security screening process, a person wearing an orthopedic shoe does not have to remove it. And I explained that the shoe-bomber, Richard Reid, and the Operation Bojinka mastermind, Ramzi Yousef, had both smuggled bomb parts onto airplanes in the soles of their shoes.

Yasmine and I had at least one more conversation. She seemed genuinely convinced that there was nothing nefarious about the men who backed-up Nour Mehana at the Bay Area Lebanese Club event. I asked Yasmine if she happened to have photographs of the men, and she did. I asked if I could see them. Yasmine said she might be coming to Los Angeles sometime in the near future and she *might* be willing to show them to me. She said she'd think about it.

BAIT AND SWITCH

In early August 2004, I had several conversations with Clint Taylor, the only other journalist who had been interviewing those who had contact with Nour Mehana's band—or at least those who had claimed to have had contact with the band. Like me, Taylor had spoken with two of the band's "promoters," only his two were different individuals than Reza and Yasmine, the promoters from whom I had been getting my information. If you add James Cullen to the mix, Nour Mehana had at least five promoters for his United States summer '04 tour—five promoters, none of whom have stories that match.

As Taylor was about to publish a second article on the band, this one for the online edition of the *American Spectator*, "Rashoman in the Skies: The Tangled Tale of Flight 327,"[32] he sent me this email:

> My article will run tonight at spectator.org, I am told. I've interviewed the promoter, Elie Harfouche, in Lebanon, and also the tour manager, Atef Kamel, in New Jersey.
>
> Elie, who was on the plane, disputes everything about your story except the McDonald's bag and the

guy with the limp. According to him, the band was
tired and slept most of the flight. He says he's going to
take legal action against you when he comes back to
the States in a month. He doesn't remember the guy
in the suit—neither does Atef Kamel, who met the
plane at LAX.

As I say in the article, the balance of evidence rests
with your version of what happened on the plane. But
I find it less and less likely that this was a terrorist
dry run and more likely a bunch of guys acting like
jerks.[33]

Elie Harfouche is a key figure in this tangled tale. Harfouche, a dual citizen of Lebanon and Sweden, apparently
also resides in New Jersey. He was a passenger on flight 327. I
know this because Taylor sent me a photograph of Harfouche
and, off the record, I verified that it was he. From Taylor, I
learned it was Harfouche who was responsible for getting
the musicians their visas—the visas that had been causing
ICE so much grief.

In his interview with Taylor, Harfouche boasted that he
had never had a visa application refused by the U.S. Department of State: Harfouche himself pre-screens the musicians
in Syria before he even starts the visa application process.
Harfouche stated definitively that one of the band members
is handicapped and that is why he wears a brace on his leg
and an orthopedic shoe on his foot.[34]

Taylor also interviewed Atef Kamel, the band's American tour manager, an American citizen who was born in

Egypt. Kamel informed Taylor that he knows of certain Middle Eastern bands out there who have ties to terrorist groups—specifically ties to the Lebanese terrorist organization Hezbollah. But Kamel assured Taylor that Nour Mehana and his back-up band are not of that ilk.[35] When asked about the FBI following the band to the casino, Kamel said, "You have to have some people follow [the bands] around so you don't leave people behind. You don't want to come over with 14 and leave with 12."[36]

James Cullen had told the DHS agents that some of the men who arrived on flight 327 "came in from Detroit and some from Lebanon."[37] And yet Kamel told Taylor that "the band first arrived in Washington, D.C., on May 30" and that he "was with them constantly . . . until the last concert at the Nile [restaurant] on July 4." I have tried contacting Mr. Kamel at the Nile restaurant eleven times. Each time, I have been told either "Atef Kamel? He'll be back tomorrow for his shift," or "Atef Kamel? He's in Egypt for two months." Once, I was given a cell phone number for Kamel (with a voice message identfying himself), but so far he has not returned my calls.

Taylor further revealed in his *Spectator* article that the rumor about ABC's *Good Morning America* trying to track down the band was not a rumor at all. Through Taylor, ABC had extended an offer to Nour Mehana and his band to perform live on national television. The band would get an all-expenses-paid trip from Damascus to the Big Apple, exoneration from any wrong-doing, *and* press unlike any Syrian band had received since—well, since ever.

They weren't interested.

With every promoter Taylor and I spoke to, more questions were raised. Some of these questions could be answered by a photograph of the band. I gave finding it one last try.

I called Yasmine, but her number had changed. For months, I visited the club's website, hoping I might be able to track down a new number for Yasmine or get her to answer an email. She never did. But ten months later, I found, posted on the Bay Area Lebanese Club website, a photograph of Nour Mehana's band from June 2004, two weeks before flight 327. It appeared alongside the heading, "Nour Mehana, Live in Concert." The photograph showed Mehana and a group of musicians. Right away, I spotted Elie Harfouche, the band's promoter. And I recognized one other man from flight 327. But the rest of the men in the photo? There was no doubt about it: They were not the men on flight 327.

I sent the photograph to five other passengers from the flight. Two apologized, saying they couldn't recollect faces from that far back. One chose not to respond. But two other passengers[38] drew the same hard conclusion I had: they recognized the same two men I recognized, but were certain that none of the other men in the photo were on the flight.

Billie Jo, the passenger who told federal agents that a man came out of the aircraft bathroom smelling of toilet chemicals, told me that the musicians in the photograph, as a group, are most certainly not the same men who were on that flight. Then she added, "Please quote me on that."[39]

So who were men on the flight? If dry runs really are going on, they need to be performed by people. And since dry runs involve testing the system, there's always a chance that the U.S. government will catch on and actually interrogate the people involved. For that reason, as one federal agent I spoke with explained to me, "it's common practice to switch out 'operatives' who are in essence working as part of a terrorist cell. Perhaps the men know little more than what they're told to do: 'Do this, do that, count passengers, stick this in the toilet, retrieve this in the toilet, try and see which one is the air marshal, see how long you can stand in front of the cockpit door.'"[40]

My opinion is that the men on the flight were not all musicians and were "switched out" when they got to the United States. "Some came from Detroit and some came from Lebanon" suddenly made sense. What doesn't make sense is that the fourteen men on flight 327 were the only musicians this side of Damascus who could back up Nour Mehana and his martyrdom songs. There was another reason they were on flight 327.

It's the oldest trick in the book: bait-and-switch. Some come, others go. Same faces, different faces. Some are musicians, some are not. Limp, no limp. Orthopedic shoe, no orthopedic shoe. Some come from Lebanon, some come from Detroit. Some know each other, some don't. Meet in the airport, identify by nods. Keep baiting-and-switching as you test the system and gather intelligence—until you no longer need any more test flights or dry runs because they've been run.

6

An Army without a General

BEFORE 9/11, few people had ever heard of federal air marshals. In fact, they were called sky marshals,[1] and there were only thirty-three of them. After 9/11, that changed—quickly, radically, and secretively. Most information about the FAMS is Security Sensitive Information (SSI), or it's classified. What this means is that few people know what rank-and-file air marshals do and how they do it. It also means that the policymakers behind the FAMS have few people looking over their shoulder and making sure their policies work.

It is the duty of the federal air marshals to "detect, deter and defeat hostile acts targeting U.S. air carriers, airports, passengers and crews." My experience on Northwest flight 327 led me to believe the FAMS was doing none of that, at least not on my flight, and so I reported on it. That reporting led to an investigation by the House Judiciary Committee. The

HJC not only began looking into what the FAMS was doing, but whether it was doing it legally.

Since its inception, the FAMS has portrayed air marshals as America's silent heroes, "unseen, unheard and unafraid."[2] But by the summer of 2004, a series of articles about the service painted a different picture altogether, one that left many Americans rethinking the reality behind the agency's façade. "Air Marshals Say Dress Code Makes Them Stand Out," read the *New York Times*.[3] "Policies May Blow Air Marshals' Cover," reported the *Los Angeles Times*.[4] "Unsafe Air Marshals," said the *Boston Globe*,[5] and these were just a few of the articles. Air marshals were in fact easily identifiable, unable to speak out, and afraid for their safety.

These articles and others revealed major problems, most of which stemmed from a huge disconnect between the FAMS's upper management policies and what rank-and-file marshals felt about the policies, particularly how they affected their personal safety, and in turn, the safety of the flying public. As these legitimate safety issues surfaced, the FAMS upper management continued to deny that any problems existed. To make matters worse, the FAMS aggressively discouraged any inquiry, about *anything*, often playing the SSI card to silence air marshals and reporters alike, of which the following story is an example.

In July 2004, I received this email from a flight attendant: "A flight attendant recently told me that a partially-made bomb was found in a flight attendant jump seat. It was on one of our new Airbus 330s that we use to Europe . . . it was in a jump seat that is seldom used because of NWA staffing restraints. I was told the flight attendants found it because they heard ticking. The flight attendant who told me this said she confirmed it later with a Federal Air Marshal who was on one of her flights."[6] The source gave me two telephone numbers: one for one of the flight attendants and another for the federal air marshal involved.

I called the flight attendant first. A young woman answered the phone. I explained who I was and that I had been told about the partially-built bomb. The young woman grew very quiet. Then she said, plaintively, "I can't talk to you. I could lose my job. I can't afford that."

But she didn't hang up.

I suggested that if she didn't want to talk to me, she should consider talking to Congress about what she had discovered. If the FAMS was burying these kinds of incidents—particularly one as serious as a partially-built bomb—the House Judiciary Committee needed to know about it. Lives were at stake.

She didn't say no.

More important, she didn't deny that the incident had occurred, only that she could talk to me. The flight attendant repeated that she couldn't afford to lose her job and added that she had a child to take care of.

Next, I called the air marshal involved in the incident. He didn't answer his phone, so I left a voicemail message. Within an hour, my cell phone rang. Only it wasn't the air marshal calling me back, it was Dave Adams. He was furious.

Every one of my conversations with Dave Adams—and there had been a handful at this point—had been heated. This particular one was off the temperature charts.

"How'd you get my marshal's number!?" Adams demanded. Then he told me to never, *ever*, call any of his marshals under any circumstances, ever again.

"Or what?" I asked him. No answer.

I was unable to get any more information about the incident, but I did pass the information on to Congress.

The FAMS continued to publicly deny that there was any evidence that probing was taking place on commercial aircraft. But the House Judiciary Committee didn't buy the party line. On September 28, 2004, in a seven-page letter to Director Quinn, the HJC demanded that the FAMS show its cards. Probing was one of its concerns, bogus FAMS policies that compromised airline safety was the other. As the House Judiciary Committee put it:

> Instances of probing occurring on flights have been reported on widely by the media, yet FAMS has stated that there have not been any credible reports of probing on aircraft. Please confirm or deny whether FAMS has garnered credible evidence on probing. Please detail the standard used by FAMS in determining whether or not allegations of probing are considered "credible." Please provide a summary of all probing allegations that have been reported to and/or investigated by FAMS and the conclusions reached upon considering the allegations."[7]

The FAMS asked for an extension to get the information together, which the HJC granted. When the FAMS finally delivered the information to Congress, my source at the HJC said that the secretive service "had to back a truck up to unload the documentation." The committee now has the FAMS information on probes. Most of it, I've been told, has been deemed SSI. Whether Congress will make this information available to the flying public remains to be seen.

—

In May 2004, an American Airlines passenger on a Chicago to Miami flight publicly outed two federal air marshals. As the passenger walked by two men dressed as if auditioning for *Men in Black,* he announced, "Oh, I see we have air marshals on board!"[8]

The incident was widely reported (it was Memorial Day and a big travel weekend), leaving millions of Americans wondering: if the goal of an air marshal is to be undercover and inconspicuous—and it is—*why do they dress like that?* But instead of acknowledging that a dress code problem exists, the FAMS boldly announced that it was considering taking legal action against the passenger who spoke up. *Dress code*, screamed the FAMS, *is Sensitive Security Information!*

One doesn't have to be a counter-surveillance expert to realize the problem wasn't the passenger, but the policy. It's true: air marshals stick out like sore thumbs. It's no secret that air marshals are required to wear a sport coat, collared shirt, dress slacks, and dress shoes on every flight.

A closer look reveals that the air marshal's dress code issue is hardly new. In 2002, *USA Today* wrote about the problem, reporting that marshals were worried the dress code was threatening their cover. "This is really dangerous," one marshal was quoted as saying. "We are so obvious, the terrorists don't need to bring guns on the plane anymore. They just need to gang up on us and take our guns."[9]

So why wasn't this dangerous policy dealt with—and changed—two years ago? Thomas Quinn, director of the FAMS, didn't think the policy needed changing. In the same article, he told *USA Today* that a good air marshal "would clearly understand, respect and appreciate the policy," adding that marshals who provided details to the press were "putting us all at risk."[10]

With Director Quinn whitewashing the issue, it faded from the public eye. But a year later, rank-and-file air marshals were still forced to stroll through airports like moving targets. Fed up, they demanded change. In a complaint to Congress in 2003, the Federal Law Enforcement Officers Association (FLEOA) stated that air marshals are as easy to identify as a "uniformed police officer." And a congressional General Accounting Office study of a two-year period (2001-2003) found an average of about one case a week in which air marshals reported that their cover had been blown. But the dress code policy remained unchanged.[11]

In the summer of 2004, the dress code issue was again in the spotlight. The question remained the same: Why do air marshals have a dress code that threatens their anonymity and puts them—not to mention a plane full of passengers— at risk? When shouting SSI and blaming the passengers no longer worked, the FAMS' brass tried a different approach. In August 2004, MSNBC wrote an exposé entitled, "Air Marshals Struggle With Growing Pains," which highlighted the dress code issue. In response, Dave Adams said the reason for the men-in-black dress code was that "we need to instill confidence and respect from passengers and crew especially if an emergency arises at 30,000 feet."[12]

It sounded absurd. In the event of a hijacking, is anyone really going to care, let alone notice, what an air marshal is wearing? Yet as Adams told the *Los Angeles Times*, "If a guy pulls out a gun and he's got a tattoo on his arm and is wearing shorts, I'm going to question whether he's a law enforcement officer."[13] Adams might ask that question, but would any one else?

So what's the real reason for the policy? The Airline Pilots Security Alliance (APSA) sees the dress code as representative of a deadly problem—bureaucracy. "The dress requirement is just one more example of career bureaucrats ignoring the pleas of frontline operators," said APSA spokesman Brian Darling. "A lot of these managers have been off the frontlines too long. At some point, someone's got to shake them and say, 'Another airplane is going to hit a building!'"[14]

One air marshal put it this way, "Director Quinn is a former U.S. Secret Service agent. What does he know about law enforcement on a plane?" Another source told me, "Quinn and his brass are not trained in aviation security and their policies prove it."[15]

The emphasis on the dress code can lead to flights being unguarded that would otherwise be protected. In August 2004, two air marshals were pulled off a flight for violating dress code rules (an airport supervisor "caught" them). The Southwest flight took off without air marshals on board. When asked about the incident, Adams again tried to play the ssi card, saying the information was classified. "Those who disclose this information do themselves and our organization an injustice," he added.[16]

The September 2004 letter from Congress called Quinn on the bogus dress code: "Do you consider the benefits of the dress code to outweigh the potential harm to individuals and mission of having an unrecognizable FAMS team? Please explain."[17]

Meanwhile, dress code wasn't the only dangerous FAMS policy that had been threatening air marshals in the field. Supposedly "undercover" air marshals were having to reveal themselves to budget hotel clerks by asking for the air marshal discount when checking in. Upset by yet another opportunity for their cover to be blown, a group of air marshals sent a letter to the Department of Homeland Security asking that the policy be changed. Adams' response? "These allegations are grossly inaccurate. Yes, the marshals have to identify themselves," he admitted, "but discreetly."[18]

The HJC addressed this issue as well in their letter to the FAMS, asking whether air marshals were required to present credentials identifying them as members of a supposedly covert team, when checking in to a hotel. If this was the case, the FAMS was asked, why?

The way in which air marshals enter airport secure zones and board aircraft creates an additional opportunity for a blown cover. Because they carry firearms, air marshals can't go through security screening with other passengers. But instead of being able to pass through these areas incognito, air marshals often walk into security areas through exit lanes—marching against the flow of passengers and drawing attention to themselves. Congress noted this ill-conceived policy and asked the FAMS to "please provide the procedures used by air marshals in bypassing security check points."

Pre-boarding provides yet another compromising situation for air marshals. During a show I did in July 2004 on KVI 570 Seattle with John Carlson, a Northwest Airlines pilot called in to share his thoughts about why the Middle Eastern men on my flight pre-boarded. "Terrorists pre-board to potentially identify air marshals," the pilot explained.[19]

In my first conversation with Dave Adams, before I wrote my first article, he had instructed me not to discuss pre-boarding with the media. I was told pre-boarding was a matter of national security. And yet a Google search revealed that the information is available to anyone who cares to read up on it. This is from a U.S. Department of Transportation,

Federal Aviation Administration memo dated November 26, 2003: "Often, FAMs are boarded only minutes before or during the general boarding process, greatly hampering their inconspicuous airport movement."[20] In the September letter, the HJC asked the FAMS to, "please provide the boarding procedures that air marshals are to follow, including, but not limited to, the timing of their boarding."

Thanks to these bogus FAMS policies, it has been relatively easy for a terrorist to determine who the federal air marshals are on a plane. Consider just a few of the tip-offs: air marshals pre-board, sit in first class, and are dressed like Secret Service agents. On a plane with three hundred passengers, anyone could narrow the field of potential air marshals down to a handful within minutes.

We might take our cue from El Al. In an interview with CNN in 2002, David Hermesh, the carrier's former president said that despite receiving "multiple threats *every* day," El Al hasn't had a single incident on one of their planes since 1968. In addition to an intense passenger profiling program, the Israel-based airline has at least two undercover air marshals on board every flight. Who they are, no one knows. They sit among the passengers dressed in plain clothes.[21]

When the National Intelligence Reform Act was passed by the House of Representative on December 7, 2004, one of its mandates was for air marshals to "wear less conspicuous clothing." December 7 also happens to be Pearl Harbor Day, a particularly auspicious day for the enactment of security legislation. It is worth noting the actions of Director Quinn on that very same day. Quinn, it appeared, wanted to enforce his moving-target dress code policy until the bitter end. On Pearl Harbor Day, FAM supervisors (known as ATSACs, or Assistant to a Special Agent) sent out memos to all air marshals informing them that if they were not wearing a sports coat and a collared shirt, they would be subject to disciplinary action.[22] Furthermore, the memo warned, teams of ATSACs would be at airports enforcing this policy—this despite Congress having said it wanted the policy changed. Here are some highlights from these "Pearl Harbor Day" memos:

> NEW YORK MEMO: Recent incidents have shown all FAMs are not adhering to dress code policy ... All FAMs transiting Washington D.C. will wear a tie.

> BOSTON MEMO: Recent events have disclosed numerous instances of FAMs from several field offices ... still not in compliance with the Standards of Dress policy. These policies have received a great deal of attention and discussion over the past two and a half years. The time for discussion is over. Compliance with these policies is mandatory, not optional. Failure to meet the standards will result in administrative action.

> MIAMI MEMO: Effective immediately, rotating AT-SACs will be assigned to and will be present in each of our airports, everyday. You will also observe that supervisors from every field office will be doing the same—assigning ATSACs to their airports to facilitate

FAM movements and to monitor professionalism . . .
they will take corrective action if necessary.

Meanwhile, U.S. taxpayers are footing the bill for ATSACs
to enforce the obsolete policy. Among the highest paid
bureaucrats in the industry, ATSACs purportedly earn over
$100,000 a year.[23]

When asked about the disconnect between new policy
and old practices, Dave Adams had "no comment." But during a December 16, 2004, appearance on *Scarborough Country* (with Pat Buchanan substituting for Joe Scarborough),
Adams did comment:

> BUCHANAN: . . . Let me ask you this, Dave, though. In
> a piece written by Michelle Malkin, an air marshal
> from the Las Vegas field office says if passengers can
> identify the marshals, doesn't that compromise their
> mission? Here's the quote: "Under the current policies,
> airline passengers are actually safer flying on aircraft
> that do not have air marshals on them. If all the pas-
> sengers know we are carrying the guns on the plane,
> then so do the terrorists—We just don't want to get
> our throats cut."
>
> Now, what they seem to be saying, Dave, is, look,
> we have got to go undercover. Like, if you're going
> to make a drug bust in Anacostia, you don't go over
> there in a suit and tie and, you know, the floor shined
> shoes and the whole bit. And can you tell us that we
> have people that are on those planes that passengers,

as well as terrorists, would not, in a second, be able to identify as air marshals?

ADAMS: Yes, I can, Pat. We have actually had federal air marshals on flights in conversation with passengers on the flight saying that they didn't even know if there is such a thing as a federal air marshal program, when in fact they are actually talking to a federal air marshal.

Adams had missed the point—again. Just because a few passengers aren't aware of the air marshal program doesn't mean the air marshals are undercover. It's safe to say that *all* terrorists know there is such a program. The goal is to fool the terrorists, not the flying public.

BUCHANAN: What about this fellow Quinn, who is apparently—they had about 30 of these air marshals come in to Reagan Airport, was it? And he [Quinn] went bananas because they were dressed so slovenly. And so what is going on? You guys are going to lose your jobs? Get the coats and ties out there?

ADAMS: That is misinformation. That information was put out by Audrey Hudson in the *Washington Times*. Director Quinn, yes, he was at the airport on Thanksgiving thanking the dedicated men and women who are flying the skies every day for doing an outstanding job. There was a very small minority of our FAMs that weren't dressed appropriately that we felt that presented a professional image.

But it's not a massive [issue], yes, we're going to take disciplinary action against these people. They just need to start following policies and present a professional image.[24]

Perhaps columnist Bob Lonsberry, in a letter to Director Quinn, said it best when he wrote, "All of us who travel by plane—or work in tall buildings—would be happier if your air marshals looked like the rest of us. If some old lady with a picture of her grandkids on her sweatshirt can stand up and snap a terrorist's neck, nobody is going to criticize her wardrobe."[25]

THE "NO-FLY" LIST?

The captain of United flight 925 discovered, once he was halfway across the Atlantic, that two passengers he was carrying were on the "no-fly" list. How was it possible for them to get on the plane? What exactly is the "no-fly" list? Who decides what names go on the list? Who checks the list to ensure potential terrorists are not boarding our planes? And most important, is the "no-fly" list working?

The "no-fly" list is one of our primary defenses against terrorist acts on airplanes. In the most basic terms, the "no-fly" list is simply a list of names—nothing more. The "no-fly" list does not include personal information such as birthdates or passport numbers. It is literally just a list of names gleaned from other, more comprehensive lists. Collectively, these larger, more comprehensive lists are officially referred to as Terrorist Watch List Information and include names, as well as such relevant information as a person's identifying body marks, where they ate lunch on their last trip to Kuala Lumpur (as with one of the 9/11 hijackers), and more. The Terrorist Watch List Information, collected by various intelligence agencies around the world, is under the stewardship of the Department of Homeland Security. According to the Homeland Security Act of 2002, the DHS is in charge of the critically important job of consolidating Terrorist Watch List Information into one list and sharing it with other federal agencies.

Any information from terrorist watch lists is considered highly classified—so classified that the people with access must go through fourteen months of security clearances to get their jobs.[26] In only one instance is any information from the terrorist watch lists ever shared with a private company—when that company is an airline. The information given to airlines is a name-only list called the "no-fly" list.

The TSA, under the guidelines of the DHS, oversees this transfer of information from the government to the airlines. The "no-fly" operates as a computer program. It is a highly classified list, hence no airline employees actually have access to it as it attempts to match names on the list with passengers attempting to board an aircraft. For example, when John Doe checks in to board his plane, his name is run through the "no-fly" list. The highly name-sensitive computer program will indicate to the agent if there is a match. If your name is spelled the same way as another person who is on the "no-fly" list, you too have earned a place on this list. Conversely, an incorrect spelling or an extra letter would likely not result in a computer match.

This is where the system runs into problems. A single Arabic name, when translated into English, can take on a number of different forms. For example, Nawaf al Hazmi is the same person as Nawaf Alhazmi, and Khalid al Mihdhar is the same person as Kahlid al-Midhar. But the complex spelling of Arabic names doesn't seem to be the only problem with the system.

Before 9/11, there was no DHS. There was no TSA. Officially, there wasn't even a "no-fly" list. Instead, the Federal Aviation Administration (FAA) acted as the liaison between intelligence agencies and the airlines, issuing what were called "security directives." Laura Brown, national spokesman for the FAA (and a FAA employee on 9/11), described it to me like this: "We were consumers of information. We relied on intelligence from the FBI and the CIA. They would send us names of individuals considered flight risks and we'd issue security directives with those names in them. That was the protocol. That was the way we got the word out to airlines that certain people were not supposed to get on an airplane."[27]

The FAA came under fire after 9/11. In his book *After: How America Confronted the September 12 Era*, *Newsweek* columnist Steven Brill writes that in the months before 9/11, the FAA's director of civil aviation, Lee Longmire, had been sent a list with three hundred names on it—names of persons who posed a direct threat to aviation security. Brill writes that two of the 9/11 hijackers, Nawaf al Hazmi and Khalid al Mihdhar, were on that list, but that the FAA failed to send the names to the airlines in time. Brill writes that when the list was finally faxed out the morning *after* 9/11, the FAA "crossed those two names off to avoid embarrassment."[28]

Brown categorically denies Brill's claim: "Before 9/11, the FAA had no separate lists lying around ... So, this whole issue of the separate lists is false. We'd [the FAA] sent [the airlines] all the names that we were provided. We had no information on the hijackers before 9/11 in terms of those people posing a threat to civil aviation. However, having said that, four of them did have pilot's licenses. But there was nothing we had from any intelligence agency to indicate that they were a threat to aviation."[29]

Regardless of whom you choose to believe, one thing is certain: the system of sharing information between agencies wasn't working. Federal agencies each kept their own databases; there was no policy in place to encourage sharing, let alone to enforce it. The CIA knew about Nawaf al Hazmi and Khalid al Mihdhar long before the two terrorists boarded American Airlines flight 77 and flew it into the Pentagon. The CIA knew the two men were in the United States and that they were dangerous al-Qaeda operatives: the agency had been tracking them since January 2000. And yet the CIA neglected to share this information with the FAA or any other federal agency. In *Why America Slept: The Failure to Prevent 9/11,* investigative journalist Gerald Posner explains:

The CIA's failure to share its information on al-Midhar
and Alhazmi blinded other government agencies when
they encountered the pair. When, for instance, al-Midhar was in Saudi Arabia in June, his visa expired. Since
he was not on any watch list, the State Department's
consular office in Saudi Arabia routinely issued a new
one. When Alhazmi was pulled over for speeding in
April 2001 by an Oklahoma state trooper, the policeman ran his driver's license through the database and
checked the registration to make sure that there was
no arrest warrant and that the car was not stolen. A
listing by the FBI on their terror watch list would have
ended Alhazmi's journey then, but without any sharing from the CIA, Alhazmi left with just two tickets
totaling $138.[30]

The *9/11 Commission Report* illustrates what happens—or
rather what doesn't happen—when information isn't shared
among federal agencies. On August 23, 2001, two-and-a-half
weeks before 9/11 and twenty months after al Mihdhar and al
Hazmi arrived in the United States, the CIA finally notified
another federal agency, the Immigration and Naturalization
Service (INS), about the two terrorists. The INS ran the two
men through their databases and discovered they were in
the United States (which of course the CIA already knew).
The FBI was made aware of the two and initiated a search but
did not succeed in finding the men in time. But according to
Posner, this was not because the two terrorists were especially
clever: "No one in the Bureau evidently checked to see if the

men were listed in the phone book. Alhazmi was in the San Diego white pages: ALHAZMI, Nawaf M, 6401 Mount Ada Road, 858-279-5919."[31]

Consolidating and sharing information is critical to counterterrorism. The information about al Mihdhar and al Hazmi was there, it just wasn't effectively collected or shared. Information sharing, which includes an effective, up-to-date "no-fly" list, is meant to be a large part of the solution in a post 9/11 world. And yet it still isn't happening.

In 2002, the Homeland Security Act established the DHS. Among other things, it required the DHS to take a leading role in coordinating and sharing Terrorist Watch List Information. The government had mandated that a single Terrorist Watch List (consolidated from the multiple existing sources) was paramount to national security. And yet a year later, in April 2003, the government's main watchdog agency, the General Accounting Office (GAO), found that many of the pre-9/11 problems still existed. *There were still nine different government agencies working from more than a dozen different lists.* Any given federal agency still didn't have a clue what other federal agencies were doing. The GAO made the need "to consolidate and share Terrorist Watch List Information" a top priority for the DHS, which is what the Homeland Security Act had originally mandated.

That was in April 2003. In August 2004, DHS Inspector General Clark Kent Ervin (the DHS's own watchdog, also known as "Superman of the DHS") released a report citing major problems with the Terrorist Watch List consolidation and sharing effort. This list, said Ervin, was *still* not working. Simply stated by Ervin, "DHS is not fulfilling its responsibility as stated by the Homeland Security Act."[32]

Michael Greenberger is the director of the Center for Health and Homeland Security at the University of Maryland. In the report, he sees the lack of a single, unified list as a fundamental flaw in the system: "You have people sitting at a desk [at the DHS] running names through six different servers. You're not getting accurate information. You can't be sure each name is being run against the right list."[33]

Ervin says a lack of resources is to blame for the misinformation—not financial resources, but people. The DHS has more than 180,000 employees, but apparently there aren't enough qualified people to consolidate the multiple watch lists into a single source. The report says experienced intelligence analysts are in short supply these days, with five or six positions available for every potential applicant. And when a qualified applicant turns up, it takes fourteen months to establish proper security clearance for that person.

The report also reveals that, in the absence of a new, consolidated, working list, the old system of identifying people who were threats to aviation safety—CAPPS II (Computer Assisted Passenger Prescreening System)—has been suspended. The pre-9/11 system flagged passengers who fit certain profiles and subjected them to additional screening measures. (Though CAPPS II flagged several of the 9/11 hijackers, none of the additional screening procedures located the weapons the men were carrying or prevented them from boarding the planes.) Granted, CAPPS II was far from flaw-less, but wasn't suspending it without having a new, working system securely in place a bit like throwing the baby out with the bathwater?

Further adding to the problems, according to the report, the American Civil Liberties Union (ACLU) has filed a class action lawsuit against the DHS, claiming the "no-fly list" violates passengers' constitutional rights, including free-dom from unreasonable search and seizure, as well as due process of law. Recently, there have been dozens of stories in the news about people who have every right to fly but can't because they're on the "no-fly" list. They include one of Washington's most recognized legislators, Ted Kennedy; a seventy-four-year old nun; and anyone named David Nelson, Mary Smith, or Kevin Johnson. (Air travelers with these names have apparently been advised by TSA officials to make slight alterations to their names. TSA spokesman Mark Hatfield was quoted by MSNBC as saying "using middle initials, middle names or suffixes such as 'Jr.' could cut down the number of 'false positives'" when it comes to being iden-tified by the "no-fly" list.[34])

Ervin's report also reveals what I see as *the* fatal flaw: lack of leadership. After reading through forty disheartening pag-es that explain why things at the DHS are such a mess (failed security systems, lack of leadership, and overall ineptitude throughout the department), I came across a memo from the man supposedly in charge of consolidating and sharing Terrorist Watch List Information. His name is Frank Libutti, and he is the under secretary for Information Analysis and Infrastructure Protection (IAIP). IAIP is the division of the DHS specifically cited in the Homeland Security Act of 2002 as being in charge of making this part of the system work. According to Ervin's report, Under Secretary Libutti doesn't believe he's in charge of consolidating the lists of information. In a memo included in the Inspector General's report, Libutti writes: "This report fails to recognize the legal authority of Homeland Security Presidential Directive—signed by the President of the United States, [who] assigns the lead role for consolidating terrorism screening data to the Department of Justice."[35]

Is Libutti in charge or isn't he? Does he want to be in charge or doesn't he? Clark Kent Ervin told me clearly that Libutti says he's not in charge.

"At the end of your report," I asked, "Under Secretary Frank Libutti says he's not in charge of consolidating and sharing Terrorist Watch List Information, even thought it is your position that he is in charge. Could this really be true?"

Ervin said yes.

Ervin also told me that "It's very clear from the Homeland Security Act. The DHS in general, and IAIP specifically, has overall coordination responsibility [of the Terrorist Watch Lists]."

But Libutti disagrees: he thinks the Department of Justice should be in charge of the lists. According to Ervin, Libutti has no "legal assessments" to support his claim. "There's a difference of opinion," when it comes to who should be in charge of the lists, Ervin said.

"So, where do we go from here?" I asked Ervin.

"For now," he said, "we agree to disagree."[36]

Three years and several oversight reports later, the DHS has still failed to create a single, comprehensive Terrorist Watch List. Without a properly informed "parent" list (the Terrorist Watch List Information), the junior version (the "no-fly" list) seems doomed to fail. And not only do we *not* have a new system in place, but we have jettisoned the old system and are now faced with a leadership dispute within the DHS that leaves no one in charge. While government officials disagree, the flying public suffers.

The *9/11 Commission Report* makes one thing crystal clear: leadership is imperative to winning the War on Terror. The inspector general's report could point out a thousand problems and suggest a thousand solutions, but what good would it do if no one is in charge? In the final pages of the report, Inspector General Ervin asks Under Secretary Libutti the same question: "Coordinating terrorist information sharing is a major part of achieving DHS' broad mission to prevent and reduce the vulnerability of the United States to terrorist attack. 'Connecting the dots' and ensuring better communications and information exchange among disparate federal, state and local government entities for counter-terrorism was a large part of why DHS was created. If DHS or specifically IAIP does not assume this interagency coordination responsibility, the question remains, who will?"

And when? The sooner it happens, the sooner we'll stop hearing officials—like Jeff Green at United Airlines—say *the information did not match up.*

INTELLIGENT REFORM?

The National Intelligence Reform Act was passed in December 2004, making the most sweeping changes in our intelligence agencies since the creation of the CIA in 1947. The need for change couldn't have been more obvious. Senator Joseph Lieberman (D-Connecticut), a co-sponsor of the bill, summed up the state of the nation's intelligence affairs on the eve of its passing by saying, "Our intelligence forces today are like an army without a general ... That will change now."[37]

Passage of the act—commonly referred to as the Intel Bill—put a number of intelligence reforms in place, including the creation of a new, cabinet-level position, the director of national intelligence. The individual appointed to this post (at this time, John Negroponte) will oversee fifteen federal intelligence agencies and will presumably ensure that critical information is shared among them. Critics of the Intel Bill say that the new position only creates more bureaucracy. But the recommendations of the 9/11 Commission set this bill in motion, and thirty-nine of its forty-one recommendations are included in the legislation. Recalling Lieberman's metaphor, we can hope that John Negroponte is the Patton to lead our intelligence agencies.

With the passing of the Intel Bill, commercial airline pilots will now be required to report suspicious incidents *directly* to the TSA. This is a major step in the right direction—a reform both pilots and flight attendants have been urging for years. Many airlines had policies in place to "intercept" this kind of information first—as in the case of United 925—much of which then went missing. With the new TSA directive, pilots will be required by the government to report dubious activity to the TSA Operations Center in Herndon, Virginia—in real time, as events are unfolding in the air.

It comes as no surprise that the airlines are not happy about this. Doug Willis, spokesman for the Air Transport Association (a major airline lobby), criticized the new directive saying it only adds "another unnecessary layer of bureaucracy" to the system. To bolster his argument, Willis used as an example the plethora of reports filed by airline passengers each day, including ones for rudeness.[38] But complaints about rudeness aren't the reports at issue, and they're certainly not the ones pilots are going to phone home to the TSA. WomensWallStreet.com, the *Washington Times*, the *Christian Science Monitor,* and other publications have covered recent, suspicious incidents involving groups of Middle Eastern men acting strangely on aircraft—all incidents that deserve the TSA's real-time attention.

As I continue to write about airline safety, I become a bigger and bigger fan of flight attendants. Not only do they work extremely hard under stressful conditions, they truly are law enforcement's eyes and ears in the air. That they have

to do their jobs with a veritable gag order in place (no talking to the press or you lose your job) must be frustrating
enough—but that they yell and scream for reform and no
one listens is appalling.

Shortly after 9/11, the Aviation Transportation Security
Act required that flight crews be trained in self-defense. Two
years passed, and nothing had been done. Even in a post-9/11
world, flight crews were still trained to cooperate with hijackers.[39] Flight attendants grew increasingly vocal through their
unions, lobbying Congress and writing to public officials
incessantly. Patricia Friend, International President of the
fifty-thousand-member Association of Flight Attendants
(AFA), lobbied Congress and made many high-profile television appearances demanding change. Dawn Deeks, AFA
spokeswoman, presented the need for self-defense training
this way: "When the passengers and flight attendants are
locked up in the back of the plane without assistance, [self-
defense training] gives us a fighting chance to protect our
lives and the lives of our passengers. The people in the plane
deserve at least that."[40]

In December 2003, a second act passed, this one called
the Federal Aviation Reauthorization Act. It gave the TSA a
one-year deadline to offer self-defense training classes for
flight attendants. Spring, then summer, rolled around—still
no classes. A group of outraged Democratic senators pressed
for mandatory security training, writing in their letter to
Commerce Committee Chairman John McCain, "cockpit
doors on commercial aircraft [are now] secured to prevent

future flight takeovers, but flight attendants [are] increasingly concerned that they will be 'on their own' trying to protect passengers and themselves in the event of an attack. Flight attendants need training so they can take steps to deter potential attacks."[41] We're talking about *training* here. Not better benefits, not more vacation time, but *training*.

Finally, on December 7, 2004 (four days shy of the congressionally-mandated deadline and the day the Intel Bill passed), the TSA offered its first, voluntary, self-defense training classes for flight attendants. At the government's behest, in five cities across the country (Washington, Miami, Chicago, Dallas, Los Angeles), flight attendants could use their time off to learn self-defense measures they might need on the job. The only problem: TSA made the announcement on November 30, 2004, giving flight attendants four business days' notice to trade days off with colleagues so that they could participate in the classes—without pay.

I called TSA to find out about the short notice: "We're early on in this program," TSA spokesman Amy Von Walter explained. "We aim to have a delivery schedule that will be released with more than thirty days [notice] next time." I asked Ms. Von Walter how participation in the program was. "We don't have numbers for you," she told me, adding, "and because it's a voluntary program, we need to see supply and demand. We need to see if it's even a popular program—so we can use TSA resources accordingly."[42]

While many pilots remain optimistic about the new TSA reporting center, other security issues remain at a stalemate—specifically the "Arming Pilots" program. The Homeland Security Act of 2002 includes a program designed to deputize qualified, volunteer commercial airline pilots as Federal Flight Deck Officers (FFDOS). The idea behind this is that pilots with firearms can defend the cockpit of an aircraft against terrorist acts effectively and efficiently, with no extra cost except training. About 95 percent of pilots showed interest in participating. The Act directed the administrator of the TSA to establish policy and carry out the program within three months.

According to Captain Dave Mackett, President of the Allied Pilots Security Alliance (APSA), "by last spring, TSA had trained approximately 3 percent of our one hundred thousand pilots as armed federal officers." In other words, according to Mackett, "after two years, only one-half a percent of our daily flights were protected by a team of armed pilots as Congress mandated." Mackett also pointed out that "training pilots to use firearms [could] protect over 95 percent of our flights. It's cheap, it's effective, and its not being utilized."[43]

Last spring, yet another act passed. On April 1, 2004, Congress passed the Cockpit Security Technical Corrections and Improvements Act to amend the law and revise requirements for the Arming Pilots program. This act shifted responsibility for the program from TSA to the Department of Homeland Security; but in shifting bureaucrats, nothing changed. The vast majority of pilots remain untrained. Captain Thomas Heidenberger, whose wife, Michele, was a flight attendant killed on September 11, put it to me this way: "It's a joke. I'm a single dad. Who can afford to volunteer to fly to a different city and stay there at your own expense for firearms training on your days off?"[44]

According to an APSA poll, Heidenberger is just one of more than fifty-thousand commercial pilots who would like to become FFDOs but find it nearly impossible to participate in a week-long, volunteer program that the TSA has set up in a remote, desert training facility in Artesia, New Mexico—four hours from Albuquerque and four hours from El Paso by car.[45]

I've mentioned six congressional acts that have been passed. But does that mean change is finally in the air? Time will tell. Time certainly seems to be something that the U.S. government requires.

7

Missed Opportunities

THE CALL CAME IN FEBRUARY 2005, eight months after flight 327 landed. I received it on my cell phone, though the number is unlisted.

"Annie, this is [names withheld]. We're from the Department of Homeland Security."

"Yes." No need to ask what it was about.

"We'd like to set up a time to talk with you."

"Okay, now is good," I said

"Actually, we'd prefer to come to your house. How is March 15?"

"Not so great. That's three days before I'm due to have a baby . . ."

They came anyway. To my house in Los Angeles. By plane from Chicago.

The four federal agents showed up exactly on time, in a rented green mini-van, carrying briefcases and wearing suits (it was 75 degrees). They came to discuss the events of Northwest flight 327. Kevin led them to our house through the garden and, from where I sat in my kitchen, I could hear their comments: *nice garden, pretty plants, too bad palm trees don't grow in Chicago.*

In truth, I was relieved that I hadn't gone into labor before the meeting. In the nine months that I'd been working on the "Terror in the Skies, Again?" series, my access to the government had been through mid-level bureaucrats and agency mouthpieces. And now I was suddenly meeting with agents (three men and one woman) who had real access to the truth—and at their request.

On the telephone, the agents had explained to me that the Department of Homeland Security, Office of the Inspector General, had been investigating flight 327. The OIG had been flying DHS agents around the country to talk to various parties: the flight attendants, pilots, federal air marshals, and passengers. They had saved me for last.

"Who ordered the investigation?" I asked. "Was it Clark Kent Ervin?"

"We can't tell you," one DHS agent said, "but it came from higher up."

"Tom Ridge?" I asked.

"Higher up than that," I was told.

So while one arm of the government, the Federal Air Marshal Service, had vehemently maintained that "nothing happened on flight 327," the other, more muscular arm (the Department of Homeland Security) had been conducting a serious investigation into it. Based on my four-and-a-half hour meeting with the agents, it was clear to me that not only had they been investigating what happened during the flight, but they had also been investigating who botched the subsequent investigation, how, and why.

So what do you say to four federal agents at your kitchen table on a bright Tuesday morning? The first thing I clarified was that, prior to my experience on flight 327, I had never heard of a "probe" or a "dry run." I explained also that I had never heard of the "James Woods incident" either.

To this, one of the agents replied, "What I can tell you is this: Mohammed Atta was one of the passengers on that flight with James Woods." This information had never been made public. With that, the agent pulled out his chair, opened his notebook (at which point the other three agents opened up their notepads, almost simultaneously), and started in with his questions for Kevin and me.

During my meeting with the agents, what was *not* said was often as revealing as what was said. Naturally, the agents "were not at liberty" to tell me anything about the thirteen[1] Syrian men aboard flight 327 (one member of the group was an American citizen), but they asked many questions regarding my "intuition" about the situation. Intuition told me something was not right, and intuition was why I began noting the men's actions immediately. And it was exactly these details in which the agents seemed most interested. One of the agents commented that I took a lot of hits in the press, that I was called a racist and a bigot simply for sticking with my gut instinct. The agents' informing me that Mohammed Atta had been on James Woods' flight seemed an indication that it's fine to trust your intuition. If you're wrong, you can always stand corrected.

Each agent carried a thick document (thirty to forty pages) filled with questions. All four took copious notes. After about three hours, they excused themselves, saying they were going to speak privately in the garden for a little while. When the agents returned, they continued with what seemed to be the same line of questioning. For the most part, they did the asking, and we did the answering. But in the course of the morning, I was able to confirm that:

- There were twenty-seven airports between Detroit and Los Angeles where the pilot could have landed flight 327, but didn't.

- The Northwest Airlines flight attendants interviewed for the investigation would only speak to federal agents with lawyers from the airline present. (One agent remarked to me, "Northwest Airlines wishes flight 327 never happened.")

- Because the men were from Syria, a country which the State Department lists as a terrorist-sponsoring nation, each man was interviewed individually by Customs and Border Patrol when he entered the country. Once in the United States, they traveled back and forth across the country several times using one-way tickets, for which they paid cash.

- Two months prior to the flight, the FBI issued a warning that, based on credible information, terrorist organizations might try to hide their members behind "P" visas—cultural or sports visas—to gain entry into the United States.

- The Syrians entered the United States on P-3 cultural visas, which they overstayed; the visas had expired by the time they boarded flight 327.

- While the men were being interviewed at LAX, none of the federal law enforcement agencies involved noticed that the men's visas were expired. ICE did not send agents to the terminal.

- At LAX, the FBI and the FAMS interviewed only the two "leaders" of the group; eleven of the Syrians on flight 327 were never asked a single question by law enforcement.

- The Syrians were allowed to leave even before the FBI and the FAMS interviewed me and my husband.

- The FAM supervisor at LAX was ill-equipped for an investigation he was in charge of, taking notes on the back of an envelope and later borrowing a notepad from another air marshal.

The agents who interviewed us that morning seemed sincerely committed to getting to the bottom of what happened on that flight. It seemed obvious that they believe *something* happened. Was it a probe? A dry run? A training exercise or an intelligence-gathering mission? My sense is that the jury's still out on a hard and fast answer. But flight 327 was far from a situation involving thirteen or fourteen hapless Syrian musicians and a case of bad behavior.

Since 9/11, the Justice Department has been widely criticized for one particular tactic it uses in fighting the War on Terror: it detains suspicious persons for long periods of time and puts them under heavy questioning before they are even charged with a crime. In the case of flight 327, just the opposite seems to have happened. There were fourteen men on a domestic flight, acting in such a way that many passengers felt their lives might be in danger. And yet not one of the individuals responsible for that threatening behavior was detained. Only two were put under light questioning—two individuals from a terrorist-sponsoring nation were allowed to speak on behalf of the other eleven. Is there a middle ground? Can a democratic nation fight a War on Terror and at the same time not curtail a few visitors' rights?

Perhaps these answers—or at least some of them—are forthcoming. According to the agents, once the investigation wraps up, the Office of the Inspector General will generate two reports on flight 327: one for DHS Secretary Michael Chertoff (Tom Ridge's replacement), which will be classified, and one for public consumption (this DHS report is distinct from the document the HJC is working on). Whether the version the public gets will be a mere press-conference account or an actual glimpse into what went wrong during and after flight 327 is anyone's guess.

As they stood to leave, one of the agents shook my hand and said, "Thank you for writing those articles." The senior agent asked if he could touch my very pregnant belly. Then he said, "As a fellow American I can say you did your duty." A third agent borrowed a line from my original article: *"If nineteen terrorists can learn to fly airplanes into buildings, couldn't fourteen terrorists learn to play instruments?"*

THE DECTECTIVE

In April 2004, I wrote about my visit with the DHS agents for WomensWallStreet. It was the thirteenth installment in the "Terror in the Skies, Again?" series. I had read numerous books, thousands of pages of government reports, and hundreds of print articles on terrorism, counterterrorism, and airline security, and I had conducted more than fifty interviews.

But no amount of factual knowledge can match the impact of memories of the heart. On flight 327, for the better part of those four and a half hours, my heart said *this is it*. Call it instinct; call it intuition: I felt it in my bones. Why the worst didn't happen will remain for me one of my life's great mysteries.

As soon as Part XIII was published, the emails began to pour in faster than I could read them. But one stood out,

an email from a man I'll call Mr. Jones. Mr. Jones, too, felt
something in his bones and, like me, wonders *what if?*

Dear Annie:

Off and on, I have read accounts of the NW327 flight ...
A friend just forwarded me the part about your being
visited by the DHS agents from Chicago.

Let me introduce myself and give you my bona
fides in the quickest and most efficient manner. Go
to the Final Report of the 9/11 Commission [NOTE: at
this point he provided me with enough information
to verify who he is and his actions on 9/11]. There I
am. I am not proud of this, and I wish I had not been
involved. I have yet to give an interview or written statement to which I am attributed, and I desire to remain
this way. I am not looking to make anything or gain
any fame or notoriety over what was just a freak set
of circumstances that caused my involvement. I hope
you understand ...

I want you to know that if you've read the Report,
I was the only (ONLY) person who met any of the 19
of them [the hijackers] on September 11 who took any
action—or felt any of them were suspicious. Although
I made my guys "Selectees," I failed to follow them to
Security and indicate that I wanted them checked further. This [following selectees to Security] is something
that is not condoned by the airline, but I had done it on
previous occasions when I felt follow-up was needed.

The reason I did not that day was because I was worried about being accused of being "racist" and letting "prejudice" get in the way. To my dying day, this will be the major regret of my life.

Could I have made a difference? Would things have been different? Is there a chance that flight could have been saved?[2]

Mr. Jones included his telephone number in his email. I called him, and we spoke for a long time. Mr. Jones was the airline agent who checked in two of the hijackers on 9/11. He was the last person two terrorists had to face before they boarded the plane they would hijack.

Before that day, Mr. Jones's colleagues called him "The Detective." That's because, time and time again, he was the one who found and removed hazardous materials from passengers' carry-on luggage *before* it got on a plane. For his stellar, security-conscious performance, Mr. Jones had received kudos from the FAA and won an award. He's the one who, for twenty-seven years, would tell colleagues and trainees what he told me: "I never want to be in a position that I ever put anyone on a plane that goes down."

And then, on the morning of September 11, Mr. Jones was faced with this:

It was a gorgeous day. There are these long, tall windows at the airport and the sun was shining through. We [the other agents and I] were talking about how beautiful that sunlight was. Then up come these two—these two last minute passengers for boarding. One I dealt with and the other stood behind him, to my right. He had this funny smile on his face. He was shifting, like he was dancing, side to side, foot to foot. He had on cheap shoes. I noticed the tickets were expensive. First class, one-way. I'd seen this before. Saudis sometimes fly their servants in first class. But usually they're nannies . . .

Here they were, these two brothers. One did the talking. I thought, *something's not right*. Then I told myself, *maybe they're just excited to get on an airplane. Maybe they've never flown on an airplane before.*

I looked at the tickets again. Cash, first class. Paper tickets. I looked at the brothers. They looked from a lower socio-economic background. They had U.S. is-sued ID cards. The cards were legitimate, though I later found out they got them through fraud. One of the brothers said, "We're going to Los Angeles—"

Mr. Jones stopped. It took him some time before he began speaking again.

I made them "Selectees." All that meant that morn-ing was that they couldn't board without their bags. I didn't follow them to the screeners. I could have—I'd done that before even though you're not supposed to. The airline doesn't like it. I didn't follow these two to the screener to request a more thorough search. I could have. This is what I have to live with to my dy-ing day.[3]

Mr. Jones shared with me the unbearable guilt he feels for not having prevented two hijackers from boarding a flight on the morning of September 11. I asked him if he was aware of all of the opportunities the U.S. government had to nab those two hijackers, but missed—all the times they could have prevented the two terrorists from boarding that flight, but did not. He wasn't.

By my count there were at least twenty-one specific, verifiable opportunities that federal and local law enforcement had to stop the al Hazmi brothers *before* this awful burden fell squarely on the shoulders of Mr. Jones. But the U.S. government didn't stop the two brothers, nor did it stop the seventeen others who boarded a total of four planes. Why? Because certain members of the U.S. government were asleep at the wheel.

In developing the list of missed opportunities, I relied primarily on a lengthy government report called *9/11 and Terrorist Travel*, which opens with this comment: "It is perhaps obvious to state that terrorists cannot plan and carry out attacks in the United States if they are unable to enter the country. Terrorists travel for many reasons, including to train, communicate with other terrorists . . . engage in surveillance of potential targets and commit terrorist attacks."[4] I chronicled this information for Mr. Jones.[5]

1. Nawaf al Hazmi should not have been issued a visa without additional scrutiny: his passport was thirteen days old. A shiny new passport presented for a visa by an individual of Middle Eastern descent who lives in

a country that is known to harbor terrorists usually indicates there are things in the old passport he doesn't want U.S. officials to know.

2. Salem al Hazmi should not have been issued a visa without additional scrutiny: his passport was four days old.

3. Nawaf al Hazmi's new passport had marks indicating he was a terrorist. (These indicators were classified when al Hazmi presented his passport for inspection—and they remain classified today. Immigration inspectors are still not provided even with declassified information about "fairly obvious terrorist indicators."[6])

4. Salem al Hazmi's passport had marks indicating he was a terrorist.

5. Salem al Hazmi's visa application was incomplete— grounds for rejection.

6. Salem al Hazmi's visa application listed "unemployed" as his occupation—grounds for rejection.

7. Nawaf al Hazmi breezed through customs at LAX, despite the fact that he was eligible for a hard inspection. (After Osama bin Laden was indicted for the two African embassy bombings, the U.S. government issued a warning that radical Islamic fundamentalists sympathetic to bin Laden were trying to get into the United States and called for "hard inspections" for certain visitors from Middle Eastern countries including Saudi Arabia).

8. Salem al Hazmi breezed through Customs at New York's JFK airport, despite the fact that he was eligible for a hard inspection.

9. As of July 14, 2000, Nawaf al Hazmi had overstayed his visa and became "out of status." He remained out of status for six months and two days.

10. The government granted Nawaf al Hazmi an extended stay in the United States, despite the fact that he was out of status when he applied for an extension—grounds for rejection.

11-16. The two brothers acquired a total of six U.S. government-issued identification cards.

17. Nawaf al Hazmi was stopped by Oklahoma police for speeding and not wearing a seatbelt.

18. Two and a half weeks before 9/11, the CIA put Nawaf al Hazmi on a terrorist watch list. One day later, they shared this information with the FBI and the INS despite the fact that the CIA knew al Hamzi was a terrorist much earlier.

19. The FBI did not check the San Diego phone book, where Nawaf al Hazmi's name, address, and telephone number were listed.

20. The FBI did not check with ChoicePoint, which had Nawaf al Hazmi's name, address, and banking information in its database.

21. When the INS ran Nawaf al Hazmi's name through its
    database and discovered he was already in the U.S., it
    didn't share this information with the airlines.

The *9/11 and Terrorist Travel* report, after stating clearly
in a few short words *why* terrorists travel, details the great
lengths terrorists must go to *in order* to travel: false passport
schemes, fraudulent visas, aliases and disguises, purchas-
ing expensive tickets—often last-minute and often one-
way—the list of complicated tactics goes on and on. And
the list suggests that examining *how* terror suspects travel
is certainly one of, if not the key to counterterrorism. The
report observes that if the government had done this earlier,
it could have seen the 9/11 hijackers coming.

The report examines the travel techniques of Ramzi
Yousef—the man who successfully built a bomb in an aircraft bathroom in 1994—to show that the 9/11 hijackers did
many of the same things Yousef did. Yousef arrived at New
York's JFK from a Middle Eastern country known to harbor
terrorists, on an expensive one-way ticket, which he paid for
in cash. Yousef used a doctored passport and had no visa,
he traveled with a fellow terrorist claiming to be a Swedish
journalist, which he most certainly was not. But instead of
kicking Yousef out of the country for not having a visa and
lying about it (never mind that his companion, the terrorist
posing as a Swedish journalist, had bomb-making manuals
in his luggage[7]), customs officials granted Yousef a political
asylum hearing. Yousef never showed up for his hearing

because he was busy plotting the destruction of the World Trade Center.

Instead of looking at the trouble Yousef went to in order to get *into* the United States, customs looked the other way. So, too, with the 9/11 hijackers. Among the techniques used by the nineteen hijackers that State Department officials, consulate officials, and customs officials might have caught, but did not:

- Passports were provided by questionable sources working inside a passport ministry office, inside a country known to harbor terrorists.

- The terrorists used 364 aliases to acquire visas using doctored passports, many of which were brand new and at least three of which had indicators of extremism (two belonged to the al Hazmi brothers).

- Visa applications were issued to individuals that had fraudulently misrepresented their employment.

- Tickets were disproportionately expensive (in comparison with those of other travelers) and were paid for in cash.

We're all brilliant in hindsight, sure, but this is different: the tragedy revealed in *9/11 and Terrorist Travel* is that the techniques terrorists use from year to year, decade to decade, remain pretty much the same. They are modified here and there, but they are much more similar than they are different.

Now, examine the case of the thirteen Syrians from Northwest 327. They were traveling from a country that harbors terrorists, on expensive one-way tickets paid for in cash, with "out of status" visas issued by questionable sources, and claiming to be "innocuous" working visitors (in this case musicians). There are far more similarities to terrorists' travel patterns than there are differences. Considering that the fourteen men *acted* like terrorists, it seems absurd not to question them, each and every one of them, at length.

ALL FOR SHOW

When flight 327 landed, more than a dozen federal agents were waiting at the gate. But the agents equipped to examine the most important element of all—the travel documents—those agents from ICE weren't there. The Federal Agents who were there, the FAMS and the FBI, neglected to interview the men separately and at length. And then, with the whole world listening, they lied about it.

Why send a posse of federal agents, but not the ones equipped to do the most critical job? I combed through an old interview with an air marshal and found the answer.

The air marshal who, right before I went on CNN, told me he was involved in an incident that made 327 look like CandyLand, had this to say when I first spoke to him:

"*It was all for show.*"

I sent him an email asking him to get in touch with me. A few nights later, he called me from a payphone in Las Vegas, using a pre-paid phone card. I asked him to explain what he meant by, *it was all for show*:

> You know how you'd go to the airport, before 9/11, and an agent there, somebody who worked for the airlines would say to you, "Did you pack your own bags?" Well, it was all for show. Those agents weren't trained in detecting whether or not someone was lying. The procedure was there to make the flying public feel good. That's what happened with 327. They all came running like in the movies, but it was all for show. Who interviewed the men? FAMS. We're not trained in interviewing terror suspects. We don't know what to look for. And the FBI at the airport? I won't go there. Who really should have been there? ICE. Period. ICE. But they weren't. Why? Because management says probes aren't happening on airplanes. The guys were there to make the passengers feel good, nothing more, nothing less.
>
> Two years ago, I had a probing incident. It may have been one of the first. After it happened, no one knew what to do, there was no protocol. The guys involved in the incident sailed off into the crowd. What was I going to do? Run up, tap the guy on the shoulder and say, "I almost shot you, now I'd like to interview you?"
>
> Instead, I filed a report about my probing incident. Basically I was told "it didn't happen." Well, it did happen. Probes have been happening ever since. I doubt anybody ever even remotely considered you'd attract the kind of press you did. But you did. That's a good thing.[8]

Epilogue

I N THE SPRING OF 2005, several newspapers again published articles about flight 327, this time focusing on
the Department of Homeland Security's investigation
into the flight. The London *Telegraph* ran a piece entitled,
"US Launches Inquiry into 'Rehearsal for Hijack' on Flight
327," noting, "the revelation that the DHS is conducting a
lengthy and expensive inquiry has raised fresh doubts about
the insistence of federal authorities that there was no threat
to the flight."[1] The *Washington Times* wrote, "the interviewed
passengers said the questioning by inspectors suggested the
flight had faced a serious situation."[2]

Both papers asked federal authorities to comment on
the investigation. A DHS spokesman told the *Telegraph* that
the Inspector General's office was holding an internal audit
and declined to comment further. Dave Adams of the FAMS
told the *Washington Times*, "I've said publicly our Federal Air

Marshals acted appropriately on that flight, other than that, I'm not going to make any more comments on that."

Whenever I try to get a statement, a comment, or a particular fact verified by the DHS, they get very tight-lipped with me. Recently, I called one of the agents from the Chicago office who had come to visit me in March. She was very nice, but when pressed to answer a question said, "I can't speak to you whatsoever!" and referred me to Washington. I called the DHS in Washington and told them I was publishing a book; I asked them to consider saying *something*. Instead, I was told, "the review is ongoing. We do not comment on ongoing work." Regrettably, press liaison Tamara Faulkner explained, she was unable to assist.

The House Judiciary Committee has been looking into the agencies involved in flight 327 for over a year. I asked Jeff Lungren, the spokesman for James Sensenbrenner, chairman of the House Judiciary Committee, if he could give me any additional information on the investigation. All he could say is that, "flight 327 remains an ongoing oversight inquiry. No decision has been made as to what format future oversight will entail."

After I handed in the manuscript of this book to the publisher, it came back with many comments. One of them was *Dave Adams must certainly dislike you*. This got me thinking. So I called Adams.

I told him that I had written a book and been given two hundred pages to say what I thought about flight 327. I told Adams that, as the spokesman for the FAMS, he figures prominently in the book. I wanted to give him a chance to say something as well. He's the mouthpiece for the FAMS, I said, not the agency itself.

"Hey, sometimes a guy has to take a sharp stick in the eye," Adams told me. Then he sighed and said, "My job is to defend the agency. To portray it in the best possible light. We both had a job to do, and we did it professionally."

Adams told me that I had caught him off guard. He would have to take a minute to think through what he wanted to say. We talked a little bit about the flight. Then he said this: "Some lessons were learned. Every day we learn our lessons. Here at the Federal Air Marshal Service, we're open to constructive criticism." He said there were no hard feelings, and that was about all he wanted to say.

I asked Adams if I could ask him one last question about something that I had suggested in the book, but hadn't yet been able to confirm. He said I could give it a try. I reminded him that both the FAMS and the FBI had said publicly that after flight 327 landed, agents followed the fourteen Syrians to the casino to make sure they were playing a gig there, then trailed the Syrians to their hotel. I told Adams I believed that neither of these claims was true.

Adams said he would have to get back to me. He said he is very familiar with the case, but he would have to verify any information before he gave it to *me*.

When Adams called back, he confirmed my suspicions. "Well, Annie," Adams said, "I verified it, and well . . . we didn't trail them to the casino. And we didn't trail them to the hotel.

What we did was, we verified the information from a third party—that the guys played at the casino and that they were registered guests." I thanked Adams for the verification and said good-bye.

Recently, I went to my doctor for a routine check-up, the kind every new mother has when her newborn is a couple of months old. My doctor and I had never spoken about flight 327; I assumed he hadn't heard about it. In the early days after the flight landed, I'd learned I was pregnant and saw my doctor at least once a month after that. Each visit, my doctor checked on the baby as he grew and then the two of us would chat a little—about books we were reading, the state of the world—this and that. But on this most recent visit, my doctor asked me, rather unexpectedly, to tell him about the flight.

So I did.

He asked me if I was bothered by the many negative things written about me. He said he'd once Googled my name and was shocked: not so much by the one million plus hits, but rather by how many bloggers suggested I was crazy.

I told him it didn't bother me at all. And I told him the reason why. Before flight 327, I used to be concerned about what people thought of me. And I used to be particularly concerned about what people thought of what I wrote.

But after flight 327, that burden lifted. After that experience, one from which I didn't think I'd come out alive, telling the truth became far more important to me than what anyone thinks of me. Simply stated, I didn't dodge a bullet to be taken down by anyone's opinion of me, including the FBI's.

In writing this book, I've tried to stick to the facts. Something happened on flight 327, that is a fact. The United States government's first and final failure in dealing with flight 327 was that it did not work with the facts—a fatal flaw in any era, but particularly during a war. Misrepresenting the truth is a perilous path for people to travel; telling the truth is the obligation of elected and appointed officials.

If the government had faced the facts years ago—that probes were taking place on commercial airlines—the government would have taken the highly suspicious actions of the fourteen Syrians on board flight 327 as points of fact. The government would have interviewed each and every one of those men individually and at length. And the government really would have followed those men to the casino and their hotel, not simply said that they did.

I've been booed by some, but buoyed by many others. I am grateful to the thousands of people who have written to me in this last year because they believed my account of flight 327. Truth matters. As Winston Churchill wrote: "Facts are better than dreams."

List of Government Agencies
Abbreviations and Missions

All mission statements are taken directly from the official agency or committee website.

Department of Homeland Security (DHS): "We will lead the unified national effort to secure America. We will prevent and deter terrorist attacks and protect against and respond to threats and hazards to the nation. We will ensure safe and secure borders, welcome lawful immigrants and visitors, and promote the free-flow of commerce."

Department of Justice (DOJ): "To enforce the law and defend the interests of the United States according to the law; to ensure public safety against threats foreign and domestic; to provide Federal leadership in preventing and controlling crime; to seek just punishment for those guilty of unlawful behavior; to administer and enforce the Nation's immigration laws fairly and effectively; and to ensure fair and impartial administration of justice for all Americans."

Department of Transportation (DOT): "To keep the traveling public safe and secure, increase their mobility, and have our transportation system contribute to the nation's economic growth."

Federal Aviation Administration (FAA): "To provide the safest, most efficient aerospace system in the world."

Federal Air Marshal Service (FAMS): "To promote confidence in our nation's civil aviation system through the effective deployment of Federal Air Marshals to detect, deter and defeat hostile acts targeting United States (U.S.) air carriers, airports, passengers and crew."

Federal Bureau of Investigation (FBI): "To uphold the law through the investigation of violations of federal criminal law; to protect the United States from foreign intelligence and terrorist activities; to provide leadership and law enforcement assistance to federal, state, local, and international agencies; and to perform these responsibilities in a manner that is responsive to the needs of the public and is faithful to the Constitution of the United States."

Immigration and Customs Enforcement (ICE): "To prevent acts of terrorism by targeting the people, money, and materials that support terrorist and criminal activities."

Office of the Inspector General, Department of Homeland Security (OIG): "To serve as an independent and objective inspection, audit, and investigative body to promote effectiveness, efficiency, and economy in the Department of Homeland Security's programs and operations, and to prevent and detect fraud, abuse, mismanagement, and waste in such programs and operations."

Transportation Security Administration (TSA): "To protect the nation's transportation systems by ensuring the freedom of movement for people and commerce."

U.S. House of Representatives Committee on the Judiciary, popularly known as the *House Judiciary Committee* (HJC): "The Committee on the Judiciary has been called the lawyer for the House of Representatives because of its jurisdiction over matters relating to the administration of justice in Federal courts, administrative bodies, and law enforcement agencies. Its infrequent but important role in impeachment proceedings has also brought it much attention."

Notes

Prologue

1   Author's emails from captains, pilots, flight attendants and air marshals (July 2004–June 2005), number approximately two hundred and fifty.

1   *Northwest 327*

1   Much has been made of this statement. Many who have been writing on the subject of flight 327 insist that the Syrians had to have gone through screening at this point; they did not. One assumes the men did go through screening wherever they originated. But the point being made here is that after roaming around the "secure area" at the Detroit airport, where connecting passengers wait, shop, and eat during a layover, passengers are not again subject to additional screening. This despite the fact that there is access to potentially lethal objects like metal forks and knives.

2   One of the men had a disability for which he wore an orthopedic shoe; the entire group in his company pre-boarded.

3   Author's husband, Kevin Jacobsen, observed this man standing in the first row of the first class cabin and repeatedly told author about the man during the flight.

4   These written notes were shown to the Federal Air Marshal Service (FAMS) supervising agent during the Jacobsens' sworn statements at Los Angeles airport.

173

5   The flight attendant conveyed this information to Kevin Jacobsen. This information was false; the air marshals were seated only in the first class cabin.

6   Aside from the two air marshals in first class, I often wondered if there was a third federal agent on board. Immediately off the plane, I watched the Asian man come up behind two of the Syrians, pull out his badge, and motion for the men to come with him. In my interviews with the House Judiciary Committee, and regarding the controversy about the FAMS on flight 327, specifically where they were seated, I asked about this third man. It was explained to me by the HJC that there could have been another federal agent on board licensed to carry a gun, but he would not have been a FAM. When the four federal agents from DHS came to my house (March 15, 2005), I asked them about this third man. They clarified that the Asian man was a FAM from the airport, someone who met flight 327 at the gate but was not on board flight 327 from Detroit.

7   Author interview with David Adams.

8   From author copy of FAMS memo from a briefing for U.S. Senator Arlen Specter, and later confirmed by DHS.

9   Author is not familiar with the actual piece of equipment that was being used. Walkie-talkie is an educated guess.

10   Author interview with four DHS agents, March 15, 2004.

11   Jason Burke, 'Terrorist Bid to Build Bombs in Mid Flight: Intelligence Reveals Dry Runs of New Threat to Blow Up Airliners,' *Observer International* (U.K.), 8 February 20. Available from http://observer.guardian.co.uk/international/story/0,6903,1143524,00.html; Internet: accessed July 2004.

12   Burke declined to provide author with further information regarding dry runs.

13   Jeanne Meserve, 'Officials: Suicide Airliner Hijackings Possible Homeland Security Warning Tinged with Skepticism', CNN.com, 30 July 2003. Available from http://www.cnn.com/2003/US/07/29/airline.warning/; Internet: accessed May 2004.

14   Sara Kehaulani Goo and Susan Schmidt, 'Memo Warns Of New Plots To Hijack Jets', *Washington Post*, 30 July 2003, p. A01.

15   Links to the original TSA memo were no longer accessible as of May 2005, although the author found this in a TSA *Post Summer Intern Newsletter* from Summer 2003, 'TSA in the news', 27 July 27 2003: "The plan may involve the use of five-man teams, each of which would attempt to seize control of a commercial aircraft either shortly after takeoff or shortly before landing at a chosen airport. This type of operation would preclude the need for flight-trained hijackers."

16   Ibid. From 1 August 2003: "The TSA has instructed the airlines to more

closely inspect everyday items that might be used to disguise weapons, such as toys, cameras, electronic devices, clothes and shoes."

17 Simon Reeve, *The New Jackals: Ramzi Yousef, Osama Bin Laden and the Future of Terrorism* (Northeastern University Press, Boston, 2002), p. 90. Many people have written and reported on the Bojinka Plot. Reeve, paved the way. Author read many sources on the subject (see bibliography) but found almost all the material was originally reported in Reeve's book, originally published in 1999.

18 See Wikipedia.com, The Free Encyclopedia. Available from http://en.wikipedia.org/wiki/Operation_Bojinka; Internet: accessed May 2004.

19 Terry McDermot, *Perfect Soldiers, The Hijackers: Who They Were, Why They Did It* (HarperCollins, New York, 2005), p.136.

20 U.S. officials and Filipino officials believe Khalifa was a key lieutenant in al-Qaeda. Whether or not he still is, is open to debate. Khalifa currently lives in Saudi Arabia. He publicly condemned Osama Bin Laden after the September 11, 2001 attacks.

21 Reeve, op.cit., p. 77.

22 Ibid., p. 79.

23 Ibid.

24 Ibid.

25 Ibid., p. 80.

26 Ibid., p. 85.

27 Ibid., p. 99

28 Department of State, Law Enforcement Report, Terrorism Strikes Russia: Summary of the Attacks from August 24-September 3, 2004, 64 slides, author copy.

29 Andrey Nesterov (translator), 'TU-134 and TU-154 Were Exploded From Their Toilets', Pravda.Ru, 27 August 2004.

30 Ibid.

31 Bill Gasperini, 'Russian Investigators Find Traces of Explosives in Plane Wreckage', Voice of America, 27 August 2004.

32 U.S. Department of State, Law Enforcement Report. As of May 2005, the State Department neither confirms nor denies this claim.

33 Ibid.

34 Ibid.

35 Wikipedia.com, The Free Encyclopedia, Available from http://en.wikipedia.org/wiki/Beslan_hostage_crisis; Internet: accessed June 2004.

36 'Excerpts: Basayev Claims Beslan', BBC.com, 17 September 2004. BBC.com notes that the information is sourced from multiple Internet cites. Available from http://news.bbc.co.uk/1/hi/world/europe/3665136.stm; Internet: accessed September 2004.

37 Ibid.

38 Stephen Ulph, 'The Islambouli Enigma', *Jamestown Foundation*, 3 September 2004.

39 *National Commission on Terrorist Attacks Upon the United States, The 9/11 Commission Report: Final Report of the National Commission on Terrorist Attacks Upon the United States* (W. W. Norton & Company, New York, 2004), p. 56. Information also sourced from: National Memorial Institute for the Prevention of Terrorism, various Incident reports, Available from http://www.tkb.org/Incident.jsp?incID=19638; Internet: accessed August 2004.

40 Ibid.

41 Department of State, Law Enforcement Report, op.cit.

42 'Arab Mercenaries Prepare Female Kamikazes in Chechnya', Pravada. Ru, 11 December 2001. Available from http://english.pravda.ru/region/2001/12/11/23396.html; Internet accessed August 2004.

43 'Separatist Chechen Chief Killed, Russia Says', compiled from *Times* wires, *St. Petersburg Times*, 26 April 2004.

44 Peter Finn, 'Hijackers Had Hoped to Fight in Chechnya, Court Told', *Washington Post Foreign Service*, 23 October 2002.

45 *9/11 Commission Report*, op.cit.

46 Glen Johnson, 'Probe Reconstructs Horror, Calculated Attacks on Planes', *Boston Globe*, 23 November 2001.

47 Author interview with federal air marshal. This marshal told author that, in his opinion, the technical definition for a probe differs from the definition of a 'dry run.' A 'dry run' being the last rehearsal that terrorists perform before the real attack. He cites the James Woods flight from August 2001 as an example of a 'dry run.'

48 Information from author interview with three air marshals.

49 Author interview with air marshal.

50 Suo Motu, Embassy of India, Statement by the Minister of External Affairs in Parliament on the Hijacking of Indian Airlines Flight IC-814, author copy.

51 In my discussion with four DHS agents at my house on March 15, 2005, the agents confirmed that individuals are not screened in domestic airports after a layover and before a connecting flight. They conceded, "this is a problem."

52 The 9/11 Commission held its ninth public hearing on 8 April 2004, in Washington, DC. The Commission heard testimony from Dr. Condoleezza Rice, assistant to the president for national security Affairs. After Dr. Rice's testimony, she took questions, one of which came from 9/11 Commissioner John Lehman as quoted by the author. Available from http://www.9/11commission.gov/hearings/hearing9.htm; Internet: accessed July 2004.

53 Ann Coulter, 'Arab Hijackers Now Eligible for Pre-Boarding', anncoulter. com, 28 April 2004. Available from http://www.anncoulter.com/cgi-local/archives.cgi; Internet: accessed July 2004.

54 Ibid.

55 Author interview with Reginald Shuford, ACLU senior staff attorney.

56 Transportation Security Administration, 'Orthopedic Shoes, Support Appliances, and Other Exterior Medical Devices,' Persons with Disabilities & Medical Conditions Information Page. Available at http://www.tsa.gov/public/interapp/editorial/editorial_1571.xml; Internet: accessed July 2004.

57 Author interview with Joe Dove, TSA Customer Service Supervisor, July 2004.

58 Remarks of Rafi Ron, CEO New Age Technology, Ltd., to the Aviation Subcommittee of the Committee on Transportation and Infrastructure, (Committee on Transportation and Infrastructure, 27 February 2002), author copy.

59 Remarks of Professor Jonathan Turley to the Aviation Subcommittee of the Committee on Transportation and Infrastructure, (Committee on Transportation and Infrastructure, 27 February 2002), author copy.

60 Transportation Security Administration directive, accessed by author at SBSTV, The World News, 1 July 2004. Available from http://www20.sbs.com.au/sbs_front/index.html; Internet: accessed July 2004.

61 Author interview with Dave Adams.

62 James Langton, 'Was an al-Qaeda Plot Unfolding on Northwest Airlines Flight 327?', *Telegraph* (U.K.), 25 July 2004.

2 *Landing on Capitol Hill*

1 Digitaria Interactive, Inc., fact sheet on page views and visits, WomensWallStreet.com, July 2004.

2 Lee Rainie, 'The State of Blogging', Pew Internet and American Life Project, 2 January 2005. Available from: http://www.pewinternet.org/PPF/r/144/report_display.asp; Internet: accessed May 2005.

3 Ibid.

4 Available from http://www.technorati.com/.

5 Daniel W. Drezner and Henry Farrell, 'The Power and Politics of Blogs,' presented at the 2004 American Political Science Association, August 2004, author copy.

6 Daniel Drezner and Henry Farrell, 'Web of Influence', *Foreign Policy*, November/December 2004, p. 37.

7 Bill O'Reilly, '*The O'Reilly Factor* for February 14, 2002', FoxNews: *The O'Reilly Factor*, 14 February 2002.

8 Seymour M. Hersh, "Mixed Messages," *New Yorker*, 3 June 2002.

9 James Lileks, The Bleat.com. Available from http://www.lileks.com/

bleats/archive/04/0704/071604.html; Internet: accessed May 2005.

10   LittleGreenFootballs.com. Available from http://www.littlegreenfootballs.
com/weblog/?entry=11733_Terror_in_the_Skies_Again; Internet:
accessed July 2004.

11   Digitaria Interactive, Inc. fact sheet on page views and visits,
WomensWallStreet.com, July 2004.

12   Thomas Friedman, *Longitudes and Attitudes: The World in the Age of
Terrorism* (Anchor Books, New York, 2003), p. 6.

13   Gary Boettcher was on the board of directors at the time; as of July 2005,
he is the president. Further information available from http://www.
capapilots.org/.

14   Author email from Gary Boetcher.

15   Author interview with Mark Bogosian.

16   Author email from Rand Peck.

17   In the twelve months that I've been writing about airline security, I've
had approximately 150 flight attendants contact me, about half of whom
I have interviewed.

18   I would learn from passenger Mark that the flight attendants in the rear of
the plane did in fact tell the Syrians to sit down, and did so repeatedly.

19   Author email from Jeanne M. Elliott.

20   Author calls to TSA and FBI field offices for Detroit and Los Angeles.

21   Later this would change; whether the flight attendent really did change
her statement, or FAMS altered the interpretation of her statement
remains unknown. During author's March 15, 2005 interview with four
DHS agents, agents told author that NWA flight attendants would not
speak to DHS agents about flight 327 without a lawyer present.

22   'Scarborough Country for July 19, 2004', MSNBC: *Scarborough Country*,
19 July 2004.

23   Ibid.

24   'Scarborough Country for July 22, 2004', MSNBC: *Scarborough Country*,
22 July 2004.

25   Ibid.

26   Michele Norris and Mary Louise Kelly, 'Analysis: Conflicting Stories
Among Government Officials Whether Syrians Aboard Northwest
Airlines Flight 327 Were In The US Legally', NPR: *All Things Considered*,
28 July 2004.

27   Author interview with DHS, March 15, 2005. The issue of the number of
Syrians on board flight 327 remains murky, particularly in light of the
passenger in first class. Author was sent, anonymously, a FAMS document
which included the passenger manifest for flight 327. In that manifest,
there are thirteen "associates" seated in coach class and one additional
passenger seated in first class identified as "not associated." By all
federal agency counts, there were fourteen musicians associated with

the incident, one was an American citizen; hence DHS later referring to the group as 13 Syrians. The math is problematic. Neither DHS nor the HJC would comment on the discrepancy in the number of associates.

28   Author notes in particular the case of Farida Goolam Mohamed Ahmed who entered the U.S., reportedly, by crossing the Rio Grande River. Ahmed was on at least one U.S. terrorist watch list.

29   'Ignoring Security Threats', Editorial, *Washington Times*, 29 July 2004.

30   James Sensenbrenner, chairman of the House Judiciary Committee was integral in seeing this legislation through.

31   '*Scarborough Country* for July 22, 2004', MSNBC: *Scarborough Country*, 22 July 2004.

32   Audrey Hudson, 'Scouting Jetliners for New Attacks: Crews Cite Suspicious Arab Passengers', *Washington Times*, 22 July 2004.

33   Author interview with Audrey Hudson.

34   Benjamin Spillman, 'Infamous Syrian Musicians Performed at Sycuan Casino', *Desert Sun*, 23 July 2004.

35   '*Scarborough Country* for July 20, 2004', MSNBC: *Scarborough Country*, 20 July 2004. Adams' information is incorrect; I never spoke to any flight attendant on flight 327.

36   Eric Leonard, 'Air Marshals Say Passenger Overreacted', KFI News, 22 July 2004.

37   Ibid.

38   Ibid.

39   Author interview with Cathy Viray.

40   Author interview with three air marshals.

41   Ibid.

42   Aaron Brown, 'Video Surveillance Surfaces of 9/11 Hijackers; 9/11 Commission to Suggest Sweeping Reform', CNN: Newsnight with Aaron Brown, 22 July 2004 Available from: http://transcripts.cnn.com/TRANSCRIPTS/0407/22/asb.00.html.

43   Author interview with the HJC.

44   Michelle Malkin, 'Flight 327 Lands On Capitol Hill', 29 July 2004. Available from: http://michellemalkin.com/archives/000310.htm; Internet: accessed July 2004.

45   Author interview with Homeland Security reporter.

46   Author email, 27 July 2004.

47   Author interview with source at HJC, August 2004.

48   Author interview with Dave Adams, July 2004.

49   Sally B. Donnelly, 'An Air Marshal's View of Flight 327', *Time*, 4 August 2004.

50   Author interview with an attorney who is friend of Arlen Specter.

51   Adams as quoted from television appearance, '*Scarborough Country* for August 2, 2004', MSNBC: *Scarborough Country*, 2 August 2004.

52   Author copy of (email) memo from Squad Five Superior ATSAC.
53   F. James Sensenbrenner, Jr., and John Conyers, Jr., September 28, 2004: To The Honorable Thomas D. Quinn, Director of the Federal Air Marshal Service (Committee on the Judiciary, House of Representatives, Congress of the United States, 28 September 2004), p.1.
54   Ibid., p.3.

3   *Reporting Suspicious Behavior*

1   Author interviews with Heather, author emails from Heather.
2   Audrey Hudson, "Second Passenger Saw Suspicious Behavior," *Washington Times*, 30 July 2004.
3   Author interviews with Carl and his daughter, not their real names.
4   Author interviews with Susan, not her real name.
5   Author interviews with Mark, author emails from Mark.
6   Author email from Charles and Kate, not their real names.
7   Author interviews with Billie Jo, author emails with Billie Jo.
8   Author interviews with Kevin Jacobsen.
9   Author interviews with Dave Adams, August 2004.

4   *Level One Threats*

1   All of the United Airlines agents and airline employees I spoke with about this incident wish to remain anonymous. I will avoid more specific attribution for the sake of their anonymity. These interviews took place July-October 2004.
2   Ibid.
3   Author interview with Jeff Green, October 2004.
4   Author interviews with David Mackett, July-October 2004.
5   Voicemail message from Jeff Green to the author, October 2004.
6   Author email from Barry Johnson, author interview with Barry Johnson.
7   Author interview with John Lampl.
8   Author interview with John (passenger).
9   Mark Hosenball and Michael Hirsh, ' Mystery Flight, Two passengers trigger alarms—and fresh echoes of 9/11', *Newsweek*, 25 April, 2005.

5   *"The Syrian Wayne Newton"*

1   Joe Sharkey, 'What Really Happened on Flight 327?', *New York Times*, 20 July 2004.
2   James Langton, 'Was an al-Qaeda Plot Unfolding on Northwest Airlines Flight 327?' *Telegraph* (U.K.), 25 July 2004; reprinted in the *Arab Times*.

3   KulnaSawa website available from http://www.geocities.com/
      kinankulnasawa/; Internet: accessed July 2004. The group defends
      itself as promoting "peace love and tolerance," not terrorism.
4   Clinton W. Taylor, 'The Syrian Wayne Newton: The Man Inadvertently
      Behind a Scare in the Skies', National Review Online, 21 July 2004.
5   This was confirmed by Cullen and several other promoters; Mehana
      was in Las Vegas.
6   Author interview with James Cullen.
7   Author interview with DHS agents, 15 March 2005.
8   Imad Moustapha, 'Flying the Friendly Skies?', *Washington Times*, 26 July
      2004.
9   Imad Moustapha created geocities.com in 1997; the site was still
      accessible in 2004 and 2005. Available from http://www.geocities.com/
      Vienna/Strasse/2806/.
10   Ori Nor, 'Syrian Diplomat Seeking Friends Among Public', *Forward*, 6
      February 2004.
11   Author interview with Imad Moustapha.
12   'Syria Halts Cooperation with U.S.: U.S. Criticisms Provoke Angry
      Reaction', CNN.com, 25 May 2004.
13   Steven Erlanger, 'Syria Test-Fires 3 Scud Missiles, Israelis Say', Douglas
      Jehl contrib., *New York Times*, 3 June 2005.
14   Moustapha, 'Flying the Friendly Skies?', op. cit.
15   Ibid.
16   Author used several sources, including: Answers.com, Wikipedia.com,
      and information from the International Carthage Festival 2004.
17   Heather Wilhelm, '"Mother of a Martyr": Nour Mehana's Greatest
      Hits', www.heatherwilhelm.com, 27 July 2004. Wilhelm used Aluma
      Dankowtiz as a translator.
18   Events Section, *Beirut Times*. Available from: http://www.beiruttimes.
      com/events/index.phtml?screen=single&link=729; Internet: accessed
      July 2004.
19   Fairouzah-American Association internet posting: 'Nour Mhanna
      Party Saturday, June 19, 2004, Pasadena, California. Available from:
      http://dorgalli.com/pictures219.htm; Internet: accessed June 2005.
      Fairouzah.com profile. Available from http://www.fairouzah.com/
      pages/805545/index.htm; Internet: accessed July 2005.
20   Author shown showtimes from the event (internal use documents)
      during her interview with Casino employees. Posters from the event
      had been taken down.
21   *Beirut Times*. Available from: http://www.beiruttimes.com/events/index.
      phtml?screen=single&link=744; Internet: accessed July 2004.
22   Clinton W. Taylor, 'The Syrian Wayne Newton: The Man Inadvertently
      Behind a Scare in the Skies', National Review Online, 21 July 2004;

also author phone calls in May-July 2005 with Amir, Tarek, and Henry, employees at the Nile Restaurant in New Jersey.

23 Author interview with Reza, not his real name.

24 Fairouzah.com profile. Available from: http://www.fairouzah.com/pages/805545/index.htm; Internet: accessed July 2005.

25 The FBI has been investigating Indian Gaming Casino and "questionable" foreign investors for two years. Author's copy of report.

26 Author interview with Reza, not his real name.

27 Author interview with Sharin, not her real name.

28 Author interview with Richard Hartshorne, member, Apple Hill Quartet, a double bassist in America who himself has played in Syria and taught master classes in Damascus, Syria.

29 Author interview with Yasmine, not her real name.

30 Ibid.

31 Jo Sharkey, 'Now Boarding, Cultural Misperceptions', New York Times, 27 July 2004.

32 Clinton W. Taylor, 'Rashoman in the Skies: The Tangled Tale of Flight 327', American Spectator, August 5, 2004.

33 Author email from Clinton Taylor.

34 I interpret Harfouche's comments regarding of the man with the orthopedic shoe and the limp to have been made in response to my suggestion that an individual wearing an orthopedic shoe does not have to go through airport security screening and therefore could be hiding something nefarious in his shoe. At the time Harfouche made this statement to Taylor, he could not have known I had spoken to Yasmine (who denied any band member had a limp), unless he spoke to Yasmine himself.

35 Clinton W. Taylor, 'Rashoman in the Skies: The Tangled Tale of Flight 327', op.cit.

36 Ibid.

37 Clinton W. Taylor, 'The Syrian Wayne Newton: The Man Inadvertently Behind a Scare in the Skies', op.cit.

38 Author interview with Billie Jo, author interview with Kevin Jacobsen.

39 Author interview with Billie Jo.

40 Author interview with air marshal.

6 *An Army without a General*

1 From U.S. Immigration and Customs Enforcement (ICE) website, FAMS home page, available from http://www.ice.gov/graphics/FAMS/.

2 Ibid.

3 Brian Wingfield, 'Air Marshals Say Dress Code Makes Them Stand Out', New York Times, 15 July 2004.

4   Ricardo Alonso-Zaldivar, 'Policies may blow air marshals' cover', *Los Angeles Times*, 23 August 2004.

5   Opinion Editorial, 'Unsafe Air Marshals', *Boston Globe*, 5 September 2004.

6   Author email from flight attendant; author interview with flight attendant.

7   F. James Sensenbrenner, Jr., and John Conyers, Jr., September 28, 2004: To The Honorable Thomas D. Quinn, Director of the Federal Air Marshal Service (Committee on the Judiciary, House of Representatives, Congress of the United States, 28 September 2004), p.5.

8   Ricardo Alonso-Zaldivar, 'Easy-to-Spot Air Security Might Be Easy Target', Los Angeles Times, 31 May 2004.

9   Blake Morrison, 'Air Marshal Program in Disarray, Insiders Say', USA Today, 8 August 2002.

10   Ibid.

11   United States General Accounting Office, Aviation Security: Federal Air Marshal Service Is Addressing Challenges of Its Expanded Mission and Workforce, but Additional Actions Needed, (General Accounting Office, December 2003).

12   Brock N. Meeks, 'Air Marshals Struggle with Growing Pains', MSNBC, 4 August 2004.

13   Ricardo Alonso-Zaldivar, 'Natty Air Marshals Discover It's Hard To Stay Undercover', *Los Angeles Times*, 1 June 2004.

14   'Pilots Security Group Supports Air Marshals in Changing Operating Rules', APSA Press Release, 19 August 2004, author copy.

15   Author interview with air marshal.

16   Scot Hiaasen, 'Being a Bit Too Visible Leaves Agents Afraid', *Plain Dealer*, 8 August 2004.

17   F. James Sensenbrenner Jr., and John Conyers Jr., September 28, 2004: To The Honorable Thomas D. Quinn, Director of the Federal Air Marshal Service (Committee on the Judiciary, United States House of Representatives, 28 September 2004), p.1.

18   Brock N. Meeks, 'Air Marshals Struggle with Growing Pains', MSNBC, 4 August 2004.

19   Author on radio show. Transcript available from Blogingham.blogspot. com/2004/07.

20   Matthew Schack, 'Minimum Crew Requirement for Boarding and Presence of Federal Air Marshals', Flight Standards Information Bulletin for Air Transportation, (Federal Aviation Administration Flight Standards Service, 2003).

21   CNN.com, 'El Al Secure because it Must Be,' 5 July 2002.

22   Author interview with air marshal. Memos obtained from several air marshals were circulated among reporters.

23   Author interview with air marshal.

24 'Scarborough Country for December 16, 2004', MSNBC: Scarborough Country, 16 December 2004.

25 Bob Lonsberry, http://www.boblonsberry.com/ Column from 15 December 2004. Lonsberry column is styled as a "note to the boss of the Air Marshals."

26 United States General Accounting Office, Report to Congressional Requesters, Information Technology: Terrorist Watch Lists Should Be Consolidated to Promote Better Integration and Sharing, (General Accounting Office, April 2003).

27 Author interview with Laura Brown.

28 Steven Brill, After: How America Confronted the September 12 Era (Simon & Schuster, April 2003).

29 Author interview with Laura Brown.

30 Gerald Posner, Why America Slept: The Failure to Prevent 9/11 (Ballantine Books, New York, 2003).

31 Ibid.

32 Department of Homeland Security, Office of Inspector General, DHS Challenges in Consolidating Terrorist Watch List Information (Office of Information Technology, Washington, DC, August 2004).

33 Richard Rainey, 'Lack of Single Terror Suspect 'Watch List' Criticized', Los Angeles Times, 2 October, 2004

34 Sara Kehaulani Goo, 'Sen. Kennedy Flagged by No-Fly List', The Washington Post, 20 August 2004

35 Department of Homeland Security, Office of Inspector General, DHS Challenges in Consolidating Terrorist Watch List Information (Office of Information Technology, Washington, DC, August 2004).

36 Author interview with Clark Kent Ervin.

37 Comments of Senator Lieberman, from the Congressional Record, (Senate) National Intelligence Reform Act of 2004, Page S10476-S10488 October 6, 2004 Available from: http://www.fas.org/irp/congress/2004_cr/s100604.html; Internet: accessed November 2004.

38 Comments of Doug Willis, spokesman for the Air Transport Association, on complaints for rudeness. Available from http://www.iata.org/index.htm; Internet: accessed November 2004.

39 Author interview with flight attendant.

40 Statements from Dawn Deeks available at www.afnet.org.

41 Senate Committee on Homeland Security & Government Affairs, 'Democrats Seek Security Training For Flight Crews, Pilots Protected Behind Locked Doors; Flight Attendants Remain Vulnerable', Press Release, (December 13, 2003).

42 Author interview with Amy Von Walter.

43 Author interview with Dave Mackett.

44 Author interview with Thomas Heidenberger.
45 U.S. Department of Homeland Security, Office of Inspector General, Evaluation of the Federal Air Marshal Service (Office of Inspections, Evaluations, & Special Reviews, August 2004) FAMS Training, p.11.
46 Author email.

7 *Missed Opportunities*

1 DHS explained to me that they refer to the fourteen men as "13 Syrians" because thirteen carried Syrian passports and one was an American citizen (purportedly of Syrian descent).
2 Author email from Mr. Jones.
3 Author interviews with Mr. Jones.
4 Thomas R. Eldridge and Susan Ginsburg, Walter T. Hempel II, Janice L. Kephart, and Kelly Moore, *9/11 and Terrorist Travel: Staff Report of the National Commission on Terrorist Attacks Upon the United States*, National Commission on Terrorist Attacks Upon the United States, 2004, p. 47.
5 Ibid.
6 Testimony of Janice L. Kephart, senior consultant, The Investigative Project on Terrorism, and former counsel for and author of *9/11 and Terrorist Travel*. When testifying before the commission on terrorist travel techniques, Kephart also stated, "When I showed a digital image of that passport [belonging to 9/11 hijacker Khalid Al Mihdhar] to the immigration inspector who admitted him ... and asked her if she noticed anything unusual about the document (she was trained in document fraud), she did not note the terrorist indicator. The irony was, I could not tell her. The information was classified and remains so today."
7 *9/11 and Terrorist Travel*, p. 47.
8 Author interview with air marshal.

Epilogue

1 Philip Sherwell, 'US Launches inquiry into 'rehearsal for hijack' on flight 327', *Telegraph* (U.K.) 1 May 2005.
2 Audrey Hudson, 'Passengers Describe Flight as a Terrorist Dry Run', *Washington Times*, 27 April 2005.

Bibliography

BOOKS

Anderson, John Lee, *The Fall of Baghdad* (The Penguin Press, New York, 2004)

Anonymous, *Imperial Hubris: Why the West is Losing the War on Terror* (Brassey's, Washington, D.C., 2004)

Baer, Robert, *See No Evil: The True Story of a Ground Soldier in the CIA's War on Terrorism* (Three Rivers Press, New York, 2002)

_____, *Sleeping with the Devil: How Washington Sold Our Soul for Saudi Crude* (Crown Publishers, New York, 2003)

Bergen, Peter L., *Holy War, Inc.: Inside the Secret World of Osama Bin Laden* (Touchstone, New York, 2002)

Brill, Steven, *After: How America Confronted the September 12 Era* (Simon & Schuster, New York, 2003)

Emerson, Steven, *American Jihad: The Terrorists Living Among Us* (The Free Press, New York, 2002)

Engel, Richard, *A Fist in the Hornet's Nest: On the Ground in Baghdad Before, During and After the War* (Hyperion, New York, 2004)

Friedman, Thomas L., *Longitudes and Attitudes: The World in the Age of Terrorism* (Anchor Books, New York, 2003)

Hersh, Seymour M., *Chain of Command: The Road from 9/11 to Abu Ghraib* (HarperCollins, New York, 2004)

Lévy, Bernard-Henri, *Who Killed Daniel Pearl?* James X. Mitchell, trans. (Melville House Publishing, Hoboken, New Jersey, 2003

Lewis, Bernard, *The Crisis of Islam: Holy War and Unholy Terror* (Random House Trade Paperbacks, New York, 2004)

Malkin, Michelle, *Invasion: How America Still Welcomes Terrorists, Criminals, and Other Foreign Menaces to Our Shores* (Regnery, Washington, DC, 2004)

McDermott, Terry, *Perfect Soldiers: The Hijackers: Who They Were, Why They Did It* (HarperCollins, New York, 2005)

National Commission on Terrorist Attacks Upon the United States, *The 9/11 Commission Report: Final Report of the National Commission on Terrorist Attacks Upon the United States* (W. W. Norton & Company, New York, 2004)

Posner, Gerald, *Why America Slept: The Failure to Prevent 9/11* (Ballantine Books, New York, 2003)

Rashid, Ahmed, *Taliban: Militant Islam, Oil and Fundamentalism in Central Asia* (Yale Nota Bene, New Haven, 2001)

Reeve, Simon, *The New Jackals: Ramzi Yousef, Osama Bin Laden and the Future of Terrorism* (Northeastern University Press, Boston, 2002)

Reston, James Jr., *Warriors of God: Richard the Lionheart and Saladin in the Third Crusade* (Anchor Books, New York, 2002)

Sageman, Marc, *Understanding Terror Networks* (University of Pennsylvania Press, Philadelphia, 2004)

Schwartz, Stephen, *The Two Faces of Islam: The House of Sa'ud from Tradition to Terror* (Doubleday, New York, 2002)

Sifaoui, Mohamed, *Inside Al Quaeda: How I Infiltrated the World's Deadliest Terrorist Organization* George Miller, trans. (Thunder's Mouth Press, New York, 2003)

Smerconish, Michael A. Esq., *Flying Blind: How Political Correctness Continues to Compromise Airline Safety Post 9/11* (Running Press, Philadelphia, 2004)

Steven Strasser, ed., *The 9/11 Investigations: Staff Reports of the 9/11 Commission, Excerpts from the House-Senate Joint Inquiry Report on 9/11, Testimony from Fourteen Key Witnesses, Including Richard Clarke, George Tenet, and Condoleezza Rice* (PublicAffairs, New York, 2004)

SELECTED ARTICLES AND TRANSCRIPTS

Alonso-Zaldivar, Ricardo, 'Easy-to-Spot Air Security Might Be Easy Target', *The Los Angeles Times*, 31 May 2004

'Arab Mercenaries Prepare Female Kamikazes in Chechnya', *Pravada.ru*, 11 December 2001

BBC Monitoring, 'Excerpts: Basayev Claims Beslan', *BBC.com*, 17 September 2004

Brown, Aaron, 'Video Surveillance Surfaces of 9/11 Hijackers; 9/11 Commission to Suggest Sweeping Reform', *CNN: Newsnight with Aaron Brown*, 22 July 2004

Burke, Jason, 'Terrorist Bid to Build Bombs in Mid Flight: Intelligence Reveals Dry Runs of New Threat to Blow Up Airliners', *Observer International (U.K.)*, 8 February 2004

Coulter, Ann, 'Arab Hijackers Now Eligible for Pre-Boarding', *anncoulter.com*, 28 April 2004

Donnelly, Sally B, 'My Life As An Air Cop', *Time Magazine*, 28 June 2004

_____, 'An Air Marshal's View of Flight 327', *Time Magazine*, 4 August 2004

Drezner, Daniel, and Henry Farrell, 'The Power and Politics of Blogs', presented at the 2004 *American Political Science Association*, August 2004

_____, 'Web of Influence', *Foreign Policy*, November/December 2004

Electronic Privacy Information Center, 'Documents Show Errors in TSA's 'No-Fly' Watchlist', *www.epic.org*, April 2004

Erlanger, 'Syria Test-Fires 3 Scud Missiles, Israelis Say', Douglas Jehl contrib., *The New York Times*, 3 June 2005

Finn, Peter, 'Hijackers Had Hoped to Fight in Chechnya, Court Told', *Washington Post Foreign Service*, 23 October 2002

Goo, Sara Kehaulani, and Susan Schmidt, 'Memo Warns of New Plots to Hijack Jets', *The Washington Post*, 30 July 2003

Goodloe, Katharine, '13 Suspicious Syrians Carried Expired Visas: Musicians on Detroit-LA Flight Not a Threat, Officials Say', *The Dallas Morning News*, 24 July 2004

Gregor, Ian, 'Officials Begin Flight 327 Probe', *Daily Breeze*, 17 August 2004

Hersh, Seymour M., "Mixed Messages," *The New Yorker*, 3 June 2002

Hudson, Audrey, 'Scouting Jetliners for New Attacks: Crews Cite Suspicious Arab Passengers', *The Washington Times*, 22 July 2004

————, 'Second Passenger Saw Suspicious Behavior', *The Washington Times*, 30 July 2004

————, 'Syrian Music Star Sings Praise of Suicide Bombers', *The Washington Times*, 29 July 2004

Jamieson, Bill, 'Is Airline Correctness Getting It All Wrong?', *The Scotsman*, 23 July 2004.

Jennings, Peter, 'Homeland Security Inspector General Loses Job After Critical Reports', *ABC World News Tonight*, 9 December 2004

Johnson, Glen, 'Probe Reconstructs Horror, Calculated Attacks on Planes', *The Boston Globe*, 23 November 2001

Knight Ridder News, 'Senate Oks Radical Change in Intelligence Community', *The Billings Gazette*, 7 October, 2004

Langton, James, 'Terror in the Skies', *The Sunday Telegraph*, 25 July 2004

————, 'Was an al-Qaeda Plot Unfolding on Northwest Airlines Flight 327?' *The London Telegraph*, 25 July 2004.

Leonard, Eric, 'Air Marshals Say Passenger Overreacted', *KFI News*, 22 July 2004

Luxner, Larry, 'Ambassador Imad Moustapha: "Syria Is Not an Enemy"', *The Washington Diplomat*, April 2005

Mackett, David, 'Pilots Security Group Supports Air Marshals in Changing Operating Rules', *eMediaWire*, 19 August 2004

Malkin, Michelle, 'Flight 327 Lands On Capitol Hill', *michellemalkin.com*, 29 July 2004.

Marks, Alexandra, 'Are Terrorists 'Casing' Planes?' *The Christian Science Monitor*, 7 October 2004

_____, 'Suspicious Airline Incidents Will Head Straight to TSA', *The Christian Science Monitor*, 14 December 2004

Marquez, Miguel, '9/11 Commission Reports: Are America's Skies Safe?', *CNN: Live From…*, 22 July 2004

Meek, James Gordon, 'Jet's Crew Called FBI in Hijack Scare', *New York Daily News*, 19 July 2004

Meeks, Brock N., 'ACLU Sues Over Government's No-Fly List: 'Innocent Travelers' Harassed, Group Says' *MSNBC.com*, 6 April 2004

Meserve, Jeanne, 'Officials: Suicide Airliner Hijackings Possible Homeland Security Warnings Tinged with Skepticism', *CNN.com*, 30 July 2003

Morrison, Blake, 'Air Marshal Program in Disarray, Insiders Say', *USA Today*, 8 August 2002

Moustapha, Imad, 'Flying the Friendly Skies?', *The Washington Times*, 26 July 2004

Murray, Mark, 'Air Marshals Train to Tackle Terrorism', *National Journal*, 4 June 2002

Nir, Ori, 'Syria Diplomat Seeking Friends Among Public', *The Forward*, 6 February 2005

Norris, Michele, and Mary Louise Kelly, 'Analysis: Conflicting Stories Among Government Officials Whether Syrians Aboard Northwest Airlines Flight 327 Were In The US Legally', *NPR: All Things Considered*, 28 July 2004

O'Brien, Miles, contrib., 'Model for Air Travel Security May Be El Al', *CNN.com*, 26 September 2001

O'Reilly, Bill, 'The O'Reilly Factor for February 14, 2002', *FoxNews: The O'Reilly Factor*, 14 February 2002

Rainey, Richard, 'Lack of Single Terror Suspect "Watch List" Criticized', *The Los Angeles Times*, 2 Saturday 2004

'Report Faults Air Marshal Hiring', *The Associated Press*, 30 August 2004

Scarborough, Joe, 'Scarborough Country for August 2, 2004', *MSNBC: Scarborough Country*, 2 August 2004

_____, 'Scarborough Country for July 19, 2004', *MSNBC: Scarborough Country*, 19 July 2004

_____, 'Scarborough Country for July 20, 2004', *MSNBC: Scarborough Country*, 20 July 2004

_____, 'Scarborough Country for July 22, 2004', *MSNBC: Scarborough Country*, 22 July 2004

_____, 'Scarborough Country for July 22, 2004', *MSNBC: Scarborough Country*, 2 August 2004

_____, with Pat Buchanan, 'Scarborough Country for December 16, 2004', *MSNBC: Scarborough Country*, 16 December 2004

'Separatist Chechen Chief Killed, Russia Says', *St. Petersburg Times*, 26 April 2004

Sharkey, Joe, 'A Case of Cultural Anxiety, Not Terror On The Move', *International Herald Tribune*, 29 July 2004

_____, 'Air Marshals Dispute Key Assertion in Flight 327 Account', *The New York Times*, 9 August 2004

_____, 'What Really Happened on Flight 327?', *The New York Times*, 20 July 2004

_____, and Damien Cave contrib., 'Now Boarding, Cultural Misperceptions', *The New York Times*, 27 July 2004

Shipp, Kevin, 'Terrorist Behavioral Analysis and Attack Recognition: A Vital Tool for Law Enforcement and Airport Security', *Professional Investigators and Security Associates Newsletter*, vol. 21, no. 4, March 2004

Smerconish, Michael, Editorial Opinion, *The Philadelphia Daily News*, 22 July 2004

Spillman, Benjamin, 'Infamous Syrian Musicians Performed at Sycuan Casino', *The Desert Sun*, 23 July 2004

_____, 'Syrian Band's Strange Actions on Flight Launch Media Search', *The Desert Sun*, 22 July 2004

'Syria Halts Cooperation with U.S.: U.S. Criticisms Provoke Angry Reaction', *CNN.com*, 25 May 2004

'TU-134 and TU-154 Were Exploded From Their Toilets', Nesterov, Andrey, trans., *Pravada.ru*, 27 August 2004

Taylor, Clinton W., 'Rashomon in the Skies: The Tangled Tale of Flight 327', *The American Spectator*, 5 August 2004

_____, 'The Syrian Wayne Newton: The Man Inadvertently Behind a Scare in the Skies', *National Review Online*, 21 July 2004

The Washington Times Editorials, 'Ignoring Security Threats', *The Washington Times*, 29 July 2004

_____, 'Mineta's P.C. Folly', *The Washington Times*, 23 July 2004

Ulph, Stephen, 'The Istambouli Enigma', *The Jamestown Foundation*, 3 September 2004

Wilhelm, Heather, '"Mother of a Martyr": Nour Mehana's Greatest Hits', *www.heatherwilhelm.com*, 27 July 2004

GOVERNMENT DOCUMENTS

Eldridge, Thomas R., and Susan Ginsburg, Walter T. Hempel II, Janice L. Kephart, and Kelly Moore, *9/11 and Terrorist Travel: Staff Report of the National Commission on Terrorist Attacks Upon the United States* (National Commission on Terrorist Attacks Upon the United States, 2004)

Motu, Suo, *Statement by the Minister of External Affairs in Parliament on the Hijacking of Indian Airlines Flight IC-814* (Embassy of India, 13 March 2000)

Remarks of Professor Jonathan to the Aviation Subcommittee of the Committee on Transportation and Infrastructure (Committee on Transportation and Infrastructure, 27 February 2002)

Remarks of Rafi Ron, CEO New Age Technology, Ltd., to the Aviation Subcommittee of the Committee on Transportation and Infrastructure (Committee on Transportation and Infrastructure, 27 February 2002)

S. 2845: The National Intelligence Reform Act of 2004 (108th Congress, 6 October 2004)

Schack, Matthew, *Minimum Crew Requirement for Boarding and Presence of Federal Air Marshals*, Flight Standards Information Bulletin for Air Transportation (Federal Aviation Administration Flight Standards Service, 2003)

Sensenbrenner, F. James, Jr., and John Conyers, Jr., *September 28, 2004: To The Honorable Thomas D. Quinn, Director of the Federal Air Marshal Service* (Committee on the Judiciary, United States House of Representatives, 28 September 2004)

Transportation Security Administration, *Orthopedic Shoes, Support Appliances, and Other Exterior Medical Devices*, Persons with Disabilities & Medical Conditions Information Page (Transportation Security Administration, Summer 2004)

U.S. Department of Homeland Security, Office of Inspector General, *DHS Challenges in Consolidating Terrorist Watch List Information* (Office of Information Technology, August 2004)

_____, *Evaluation of the Federal Air Marshal Service* (Office of Inspections, Evaluations, & Special Reviews, August 2004)

U.S. Department of State, Overseas Security Advisory Council, *Terrorism Strikes Russia: Summary of the Attacks from August 24—September 3, 2004*, Law Enforcement Report (U.S. Department of State, Autumn 2004)

United States General Accounting Office, *Information Technology: Terrorist Watch Lists Should Be Consolidated to Promote Better Integration and Sharing*, Report to Congressional Requesters (General Accounting Office, April 2003)

_____, Aviation Security: *Federal Air Marshal Service Is Addressing Challenges of Its Expanded Mission and Workforce, but Additional Actions Needed,* (General Accounting Office, December 2003)

A NOTE ON THE AUTHOR

ANNIE JACOBSEN is a journalist and writer for WomensWallStreet.com. Her work on business, finance, and terrorism has appeared in a variety of national and international magazines and webzines. A graduate of Princeton University, she lives in Los Angeles, California, with her husband and two sons.

This book was designed and set into type
by Mitchell S. Muncy,
with cover design by Stephen J. Ott,
and printed and bound
by Bang Printing,
Brainerd, Minnesota.

℃

The text face is Minion Multiple Master,
designed by Robert Slimbach
and issued in digital form by Adobe Systems,
Mountain View, California, in 1991.

℃

The paper is acid-free and is of archival quality.

42